Ideations in the Dark

A Spiritual Framework for Healing Depression and Suicidal Thoughts

Walter K Stewart

Stewart Solutions Press

Preface

Thirty years ago, my world collapsed.

What began as a nervous breakdown quickly became something far more consuming as severe depression that wrapped itself around my thoughts, emotions, and sense of identity. It felt like living at the bottom of a pit: dark, frightening, and inescapable. In that place, I faced a decision that many people will recognize as both frightening and deeply personal. I chose to trust that God would help me rather than relying on prescription medication for my diagnosis.

I didn't make that choice out of denial or pride. I made it because something in me needed to know whether spiritual alignment with the Creator could produce mental and emotional restoration. It took a while, and it did help representing one of the best decisions of my life.

God's process helped me heal mentally and spiritually. Not in a way that erased the struggle overnight, but in a way that gave me direction, endurance, and ultimately, a path forward. During those desperate hours when everything felt uncertain, I made a promise to myself: if I survived, I would one day understand what happened to me.

I would learn the mechanics of my healing through God's process, and I would share what I learned with others especially those who are searching for a spiritual purpose while fighting to stay alive. That promise is why this book exists. This book isn't a theory. It was survival.

Ideations in the Dark: A Spiritual Framework for Healing Depression and Suicidal Thoughts was written to solve a specific problem: when a person is trapped in depression and haunted by suicidal thoughts, they often don't need more vague encouragement but a clear path. They need language for what they're experiencing and the steps they can practice when their mind feels ungovernable. They need a way to regain stability, rebuild hope, and re-enter life with purpose.

This book is my attempt to offer that path a prescription rooted in spiritual alignment, strengthened by real-world experience, and designed to be practical. My credibility comes from both suffering and service. I lived with severe depression for seven years before I was ready to climb out of the Place in Time (PIT) where life narrows, pain intensifies, and the mind feels like a prison. I know what it is to endure day after day when "getting through the day" feels like the only goal. I also know that healing often requires more than one kind of support.

During my journey, I was fortunate to undergo many therapy sessions with licensed professionals, including the Veterans Administration. That help mattered. It provided a foundation of understanding, structure, and support that strengthened my ability to recover.

As I rebuilt my life, I felt compelled to help others who were standing in the same shadows. I served as a bereavement counselor with the Contra

Costa Crisis Center in Walnut Creek, California, where I facilitated group sessions and made home visits meeting people in the rawest moments of grief and despair. I also delivered a suicide prevention presentation at UC Berkeley during the Annual East Bay High School Convention, speaking directly to the reality that young people, too, carry unbearable pain in silence.

Serving in the U.S. Air Force and U.S. Air Force Reserves afforded me the opportunity to work in the Airman & Family Readiness Center. As the Assistant Non-Commissioned Officer in Charge, I conducted suicide prevention workshops for hundreds of new Air Force recruits teaching not only warning signs and intervention tools, but the deeper truth that strength includes reaching for help.

Through Saddleback Church, I attended several years of their mental health summits and obtained my suicide prevention certification. I also completed their extensive counseling program, which covered many areas including depression and suicide prevention. I also served as the Human Relations Commissioner for Contra Costa County where I supported the public through traumatic events.

Over time, my lived experience and my professional service began to converge into a single burden and a single calling: to translate pain into guidance. The journey to write this book took time to understand the healing process while cultivating a deeper understanding of my own spiritual path. Some breakthroughs arrive in a moment; most arrive through a process. And my process included a turning point that still stands out as both literal and spiritual.

One day I picked up a hitchhiker on a freeway onramp in Oakland, California. After a two-hour drive through darkness and rain, I invited him to stay and overnight with me for the evening. The next twenty-four hours would change my life forever. He told me that he had planned to commit suicide if no one picked him up. His solemn prayer to God became my call to answer the spirit.

That encounter led me to discover my spiritual purpose and to understand something I hadn't fully grasped before that the pain we survive is transmutable. It can be transformed. I started to understand that my journey could help someone else choose to live beyond their pain.

It took me thirty years to write **Ideations in the Dark** because I believe God needed time to give me the right prescription for overcoming my pain until I could finally recognize, practice, and articulate it in a way which could serve others.

This book is not rushed advice. It is distilled experience. It is a map drawn from the inside of the PIT.

This book is for adults and mature teenagers who have endured traumatic events and now feel shackled by deep depression struggling to control their thoughts and emotions, somehow feeling trapped in a cycle of hopelessness. It's also for those who have considered suicide as an escape from pain.

It can also benefit those who desire a nonreligious orientation but open to spiritual alignment and may not identify with organized religion, yet still sense that healing involves more than chemistry, circumstance, or willpower alone.

Within these pages, you can expect a practical guide built around resilience, self-assessment, and actionable steps designed to help you climb out of the deepest darkness. The goal isn't to shame you for being in pain or to minimize what you've endured. The goal is to help you release the pain, regain stability, and develop the courage to accept that your life may still be guided by a larger plan that includes restoration, purpose, and a future you cannot yet see.

I also want to offer gratitude, because no one makes it through darkness alone. There are many people to whom I owe deep gratitude and thanks for helping me survive the toughest seasons of my life and for helping me live my best life while completing this mission. To my best friend and Air Force buddy Milt, thank you for standing with me when I didn't have the strength to stand on my own. Thank you for the forty years of great friendship.

And to my beautiful amazing wife Ash, my breakthrough blessing and my dream maker, thank you for loving and completing me. You helped me keep believing in a new chapter long before I could fully see it. You've always echoed God's sentiment. I am so grateful.

If you are reading this and you feel like you're still in the PIT, I want you to hear me clearly: *you are not alone, and you are not beyond help.*

This book was written for you by someone who has lived in that darkness and found a way out through God's process.

Introduction

Don't handle it alone. Don't suffer in silence. Not because you're incapable, but because you were never designed to carry this kind of weight in isolation.

If you're reading this, I'm going to assume something simple and true: you've been carrying more than you've been saying out loud. Maybe you've been functioning showing up, paying bills, doing the basic things that make life look normal from the outside while inside, something has been slipping. Or maybe you haven't been functioning at all, and you're exhausted from trying to explain what it feels like to be "stuck" in your own mind.

Depression has a way of shrinking the world until the simplest things feel like a test you didn't study for. Getting out of bed can feel like lifting a weight that isn't there. Conversations can feel like noise you're expected to translate. Smiles can feel like obligations. And sleep can become either a stranger or a hiding place.

And when suicidal thoughts show up, they don't always arrive as panic. Sometimes they arrive as persuasion. Sometimes they arrive as a quiet, convincing suggestion that sounds like relief. That's what makes them so dangerous: they come wearing the voice of logic when you're too tired to argue. They show up when your body is depleted, when your spirit is bruised, when your mind has been running emergency drills for too long. They whisper, "This is the only way to stop hurting."

If that's familiar, I want you to hear this plainly:

You're not a bad person for having those thoughts.
You're not weak for being tired.
And you're not alone for feeling that way.

Your pain deserves compassion, not judgment. Your struggle deserves support, not secrecy. There is no honor in suffering quietly if help is available. And even when help feels far away, there are still steps you can take steady, real steps that move you toward safety, stability, and meaning again.

This book exists because there is a moment sometimes quiet, sometimes dramatic when the soul reaches a line in the sand and says, "I can't keep living like this. "Not as a threat, but as a truth. And right after that truth, another truth becomes possible: "Maybe I can live differently."

That second sentence is what I call an ideation worth keeping.

Depression doesn't just change your mood. It changes your interpretation of reality. It changes what your mind calls "evidence." It changes how you hear your own thoughts. It can distort memory, motivation, appetite, sleep, self-worth, and your sense of time. It can convince you that the best parts of your life are behind you and that the future is either blank or hostile.

If you've ever looked in the mirror and felt like you were looking at someone you don't recognize, you know what I mean. The mind becomes a battlefield, and you're not just fighting feelings you're fighting conclusions. That's why "just thinking positive" doesn't work. That's why shame doesn't heal anyone. That's why this book is not a lecture or a performance. It is a process. A road with landmarks. A guide for people who are trying to find their way back to themselves and, if you're open to it, back to God.

I'm going to speak about God the divine in these pages. Not as a debate topic. Not as a weapon. Not as a label. I mean God as presence, guidance, mercy, timing, and the kind of help that shows up when you can't manufacture strength on demand.

If you're wary of spiritual language, I respect that. Some people have been harmed by religion. Some people have been dismissed with spiritual clichés when they needed real compassion. Some people have prayed and still suffered, and they don't know what to do with that. This book is not here to pressure you into a version of faith that ignores reality. This book is here to offer a gentle, steady truth:

God can meet you in reality.

Not after you clean yourself up. Not after you become "strong again." Not after you stop struggling but during the struggle within the confines of the PIT.

Throughout this book, you'll see me use the phrase: PIT your *Place in Time*. The PIT is not a diagnosis. It's a season. A psychological and spiritual location where life narrows, and everything feels heavier than it should. It is a place where there is an energy shift between the internal landscape and the external environment which impacts the collaboration between the mind and spirit.

The PIT can be the season after a loss, a betrayal, a divorce, a breakdown, a failure, a trauma, an illness, a series of disappointments, or simply a long stretch of living without the nourishment your soul needs. Sometimes the PIT begins with one major event. Sometimes it begins with a thousand small cuts you kept accepting and tolerating.

The PIT is the place where you're forced to reckon with yourself, patterns, wounds, beliefs, coping strategies, fears, and the silent stories you've been carrying. It's also the place where your relationship with God can feel complicated. Some people feel angry and abandoned. Some feel numb or guilty. And then there are others who feel nothing at all and simply don't know how to pray.

If that's where you are, you haven't failed. You're simply in a place where old answers don't work.

Here is what I have learned, slowly and sometimes painfully:

The PIT may seem like punishment; but it transforms into an incubator.

An incubator isn't comfortable. It isn't glamorous. It's a protected environment where something fragile gets stabilized and strengthened until it can live in the open again. The PIT can be like an enclosed season where God begins rebuilding what life has shaken, where your spirit begins to gather itself, where your inner world is restructured with more honesty than you've ever had before.

You may not have chosen the PIT. But you can choose what you do inside it and overtime you will decide how long you'll need to stay.

When people talk about breakthroughs, they often imagine a dramatic moment: a sudden lifting, a powerful spiritual experience, an instant turnaround. Those moments can happen. But I don't want to build your hope on the idea that healing must arrive like fireworks.

Sometimes breakthroughs are quiet.

Sometimes it's the day you finally tell the truth to someone safe.

Sometimes it's the moment you admit you need help and you stop treating that admission like a failure.

Sometimes it's the decision to do one small thing consistently, even when you don't feel like it.

Sometimes it's the realization that your thoughts are not commands but signals.

Breakthrough can be a turning point, yes, but it's often a pattern: a series of choices that slowly shifts the direction of your life. You don't always feel it is happening. You just notice one day that the darkness doesn't have the same authority it used to. The PIT is still the PIT, but you're standing differently inside it. Your spirit is no longer succumbed to the pain.

This is what I mean by spiritual readiness: not hype, not denial, not pretending you feel great. Spiritual readiness is the quiet capacity to keep your heart open to change even when your emotions are uncooperative. It's the willingness to believe that God is still working even when you can't see evidence yet. And sometimes breakthroughs can be provisions you didn't predict. What could be a moment when the unexpected door opens, the right person in the right place, an inspirational conversation, the resource you didn't know existed, the sentence that lands in your heart at the right time and keeps you from making the wrong decision.

Some people call it a coincidence. I don't. I call it "divine intervention."

I wrote this book because I understand the tension between wanting peace and not knowing how to reach it. I understand the exhaustion of trying to keep functioning while your inner life is unraveling. I understand the feeling of being tired of yourself not because you hate yourself, but because you don't know how to stop hurting. And I wrote this because I've lived long enough to see something else: pain can be honest without being permanent. Darkness can be real without being final.

This book is for people who are fighting quietly. People who have done therapy and still feel stuck. People who can't access therapy at all. People who are undiagnosed. People who have tried medication or don't want medication. People who are spiritually hungry but emotionally depleted. People who are functioning enough that nobody checks on them and suffering enough that they secretly hope someone does.

If you're in that space, I want you to have a roadmap. Not a rigid formula. A roadmap, options, tools, perspective, and a spiritual thread strong enough to hold you when you feel like you can't hold yourself. This is exactly what I needed to understand some thirty years ago.

You'll notice that I respect clinical care in this book. Because I've seen it help. Psychotherapy, cognitive behavioral therapy, medication, structured programs, and crisis services are not signs of spiritual failure. For many people, they are instruments of healing. Mental health treatment is an evidenced based structured process aimed at diagnosing and treating mental illnesses, emotional distress, and behavior issues delivered by licensed mental health professionals.

If you need help, you deserve help. If your mind is in danger, your safety matters more than your pride. If your thoughts have become threatening, your next step is not to "tough it out." Your next step is to reach out immediately.

This book offers spiritual comfort and practical stability, but it does not replace professional care when professional care is needed. Sometimes the holiest thing you can do is make a call to the helpline. Sometimes courage looks like telling someone, "I'm not okay."

This book begins with a choice most people don't realize they have until they're exhausted: the choice between approaches clinical, nonclinical, and a wise blend of both.

Clinical tools matter. Psychotherapy (Talk Therapy). Cognitive Behavioral Therapy. Medication (FDA-approved and off-label). Brain stimulation therapies. Imaging and research that help clinicians understand the signaling within the brain.

And yes, there are conversations about Ketamine now, too. A term I learned during my time at California State University Los Angeles Biotechnology Program (BIOSTART). Our cohort was mostly medical doctors, PhD's, scientists, psychologists, psychiatrists, and post-doctoral students who were founders focused on developing novel drug discoveries as FDA Approved pharmaceutical and medical device companies.

I was fortunate to be accepted into the highly competitive BIOSTART Program, bringing with me a Master of Business Administration and a Bachelor of Science in Professional Aeronautics. The opportunity represented an unexpected convergence of disciplines, allowing me to apply both business acumen and analytical problem-solving skills within an entirely new field.

We were emersed in the biotechnology ecosystem to include the drug discovery approval process, intellectual property discussions, technology transfers, and industry affiliations such as BIOCOM. This bootcamp taught us all aspects of delivering revolutionary businesses to help humans thrive with science and technology.

I was keenly interested in Ketamine itself as a FDA-approved as an anesthetic, while Esketamine (Spravato) is FDA-approved for specific depression indications under medical supervision. Esketamine is primarily used for Treatment Resistant Depression (TRD) and has proven success with helping people who suffer from suicidal ideations.

I learned that most depression drugs affect the neurotransmitter functions of the brain. So, if you are considering taking prescription medications for depression, then you should familiarize yourself with the pharmaceuticals. You don't need to become a neuroscientist, but learning a few basic terms can help you ask better questions and make decisions with clarity. You should familiarize yourself with four brain messengers: glutamate, serotonin, norepinephrine, and dopamine.

For some people, part of healing includes clinical support, therapy, structured care, and sometimes medication. There is no shame in that. If you're considering prescription treatment, I want you to feel informed, not overwhelmed.

Neurotransmitters are chemical messengers your brain uses to send signals. You don't need to memorize biology terms. You just want enough familiarity to ask good questions about the side-effects and recognize what your clinician is talking about.

Serotonin — the "steady mood" messenger is often linked to emotional balance, anxiety, sleep, and appetite. When people talk about feeling "more even" or less emotionally reactive, serotonin is often part of that conversation. Many common antidepressants are designed to increase serotonin signaling over time.

Norepinephrine — the "energy and focus" messenger is tied to alertness, attention, and the body's stress response. When depression looks like heavy fatigue, low drive, brain fog, or feeling unable to "get going," norepinephrine may be involved. Some medications aim to support this system to improve energy and concentration.

Dopamine — the "motivation and reward" messenger is connected to motivation, pleasure, and the ability to feel interest or enjoyment. When depression steals your spark and nothing feels rewarding, and even good things feel flat dopamine is often part of the picture. Certain treatments are chosen specifically when low motivation and emotional "numbness" are major symptoms.

Glutamate — the "learning and brain connection" messenger is the brain's most common excitatory neurotransmitter and plays a major role in learning, memory, and neuroplasticity. In recent years, glutamate has gained attention because some newer depression treatments target glutamate pathways differently than traditional antidepressants. This is part of why ketamine-based treatments are discussed in treatment-resistant depression under medical supervision.

Neurotransmitters are only one part of the story. Depression is not caused by a single "chemical imbalance," and medication decisions should be made with a qualified clinician who can consider your symptoms, history, risks, and overall health. But learning these basics can help you feel less intimidated and more empowered when you talk about treatment options.

Nonclinical tools matter, too. Structure. Ritual. Community. Boundaries. Purpose. Honest spiritual practice. The daily choices that don't sound dramatic but quietly keep you alive.

The point isn't to pick a "team." The point is to stop suffering in silence while you try to muscle your way back to stability.

Clinically, depression gets defined using diagnostic criteria, symptom clusters, duration, and severity. Major Depressive Disorder is often described in terms of depressed mood, loss of interest, sleep disruption, low energy, hopelessness, impaired concentration, changes in appetite, feelings of worthlessness, and sometimes suicidal thoughts.

But on the inside, it's not a list. It's a lived experience.

It can last weeks, months, or some people, years sometimes recurring lingering like a shadow that won't leave. And the longer it stays, the more it tries to convince you that this is your identity instead of your condition.

Depression also has a way of isolating you, even when you're surrounded. It tells you, "Don't burden anyone." It tells you, "You should be over this by now." and "If people really knew, they'd leave."

That's why I'm starting with the sentence I want you to repeat until it doesn't feel strange anymore: *Don't handle it alone. Don't suffer in silence.*

I'm writing from both sides of the struggle.

On the personal side: I know severe depression from the inside. I know what it means when your mind starts trying to bargain with life. I know isolation, exhaustion, internal debates, and the fear of being honest about what you're thinking. An over the years, I've lost several family and friends to suicide. My pain inspired me to write this book because I didn't understand the impact or how depression affected the mechanics within my brain.

On the professional side: I have served in roles that required me to sit with crisis, grief, and the realities of suicidal pain supporting individuals and families as they tried to make sense of what felt senseless. I've learned what helps, harms, comforts, and what pushes people further into silence. I followed this path to unpack my own pain.

For many years in the Air Force, I performed suicide prevention workshops for hundreds of new recruits for the Airman Readiness Center at

Travis Air Force Base in California. I also served as a volunteer at Contra Costa Crisis Center in Walnut Creek, California for several years, making home visits and facilitating bereavement group sessions. I also made presentations at the Annual East Bay High School Convention at UC Berkeley to hundreds of high school students.

In addition, I graduated from Saddleback Church's Counseling Program located in Lake Forest, California where I was exposed to many topics including depression and suicidal ideations. I attended the annual mental health summit for several years where I obtained my suicide awareness certificate. Overall, I've spent countless years conversing with people in pain even as a Human Relations Commissioner for Contra Costa County.

So when I speak, I'm not speaking like an expert or someone above you. I'm speaking as someone who has been close enough to this kind of pain to respect it. This book was written as a companion and a resource to help you navigate this difficult journey.

This book will help you do four things that depression tries to steal:

Clarity: You'll learn to name what's happening emotionally, mentally, spiritually so you're no longer fighting a shadow.

Stability: You'll develop simple patterns, rituals, and inner practices that help anchor you when mood and thought patterns swing.

Agency: You'll reclaim the power to choose your next step, even when you can't choose how you feel.

Alignment: You'll begin aligning your spirit and purpose so life becomes more than survival, and your future becomes visible again.

The goal is not perfection. The goal is movement. The goal is not "never feel sad again." The goal is to learn how to stand when sadness shows up.

This book is organized into four sections and eighteen chapters in total. Think of these sections as stages of moving from understanding your PIT experience to rebuilding your life with in it and climbing out when you're finally ready.

Part One: Prescription
This is where we name the PIT and learn what it means to live inside a hard season without surrendering to it. We talk about navigating the darkness, reckoning with yourself and God, and building stabilizing practices that help you hold your ground.

Part Two: Overcoming
This is where we develop courage and spiritual readiness and the ability to keep showing up with an expectant spirit, even when emotions fluctuate. This section is about what it means to fight wisely, not violently; steadily, not dramatically.

Part Three: Depression
This is where we go deeper into the solitary path, renewing the mind, and recognizing the power you still have to change. Depression tries to convince you that you are powerless. This section challenges the misconception with truth and practice while reclaiming agency.

Part Four: Suicidal Thoughts
This is where we speak openly about what many people hide. We explore intimacy with God, aligning spirit and purpose, discovering an illuminated path, surrendering to destiny, and most importantly choosing life. Not once, but repeatedly. Choosing life as a practice. Choosing life as a spiritual act.

And woven through all of it is one steady truth:

You don't have to handle it alone. You don't have to suffer in silence.

Before we begin, I want to speak to the person who is reading this with a quiet fear: "I don't know if I'm going to make it."

If that's you, please pause and do one brave thing: tell someone safe what's going on. Call a crisis line. Reach out to a counselor, a friend, a family member, a pastor, a doctor or someone who can respond with care. If you are in immediate danger in the U.S., you can call or text 988 right now.

There is no shame in needing help. There is only wisdom in staying alive.

Let this be the beginning.

You don't have to solve your whole life today.

You don't have to understand everything right now.

You don't have to feel strong before you take a step.

You only have to do the next right thing.

You only have to put one foot in front of the other to keep walking.

This book is your invitation back to yourself steadily, honestly and if you're willing, back with God's guidance, mercy, and timing. The PIT may be where you are, but it does not have to be where you remain.

Don't handle it alone. Don't suffer in silence.

Let's begin.

Disclaimer

Ideations in the Dark is a work of personal memoir, spiritual reflection, and faith-based encouragement. It is written from the author's own lived experience and is offered in the spirit of honest witness, not professional guidance.

This book contains frank discussion of depression, suicidal thought, grief, and emotional crisis. These topics are addressed with care and with the sincere intention of offering hope to those who may be navigating similar experiences. However, nothing in this book is intended to serve as a substitute for professional mental health care, medical treatment, or crisis intervention.

If you or someone you know is experiencing suicidal thoughts, emotional crisis, or a mental health emergency, please reach out to a qualified professional immediately. In the United States, you can call or text **988** at any time to reach the Suicide and Crisis Lifeline, where trained counselors are available twenty-four hours a day, seven days a week.

The author's experience of choosing faith over prescription medication in his own journey is personal and specific to his circumstances. It is not a recommendation for others to follow the same path. Every individual's mental health needs are unique, and professional medical and psychological support can be essential and life-saving. Please seek qualified help when you need it.

The stories of others referenced in this book have been shared with care for their dignity.

This book is offered as testimony, not prescription as one person's account of what the darkness looks like from the inside, and what it looks like from the other side of it.

Table of Contents

PART ONE

Prescription

Sometimes being in the PIT is the prescription.

When you are trapped in the darkness of the PIT, your immediate, desperate instinct is to look for an escape hatch. You open a book like this looking for a fast-acting spiritual anesthetic—a quick way out, a sovereign eviction notice for your pain, or a checklist to bypass the suffering entirely.

True structural repair doesn't work that way. Have done worked in the construction field I know that you can never fix a fractured foundation by simply painting over the cracks in the drywall; you have to dig down into the dirt where the shift occurred. Sometimes, the heavy, suffocating confinement of the PIT is not a sign that your life has failed, but rather it is the exact script written for your restoration. The darkness itself is the medicine.

To understand this, we have to look through the lens of a Master Builder and look at the blueprint of construction. Before a magnificent new tower can pierce the skyline, a massive, gaping hole must first be carved into the earth. The deeper the building is destined to rise, the deeper and more jarring the initial excavation must be. This isn't a sign of divine abandonment or system failure; it is a deliberate, calculated demolition.

Drawing from the principles of spiritual care I've come to understand we must learn to see that God often uses the weight of the PIT to clear out the toxic, unstable debris of our old ways of thinking. The excavation hurts, and the open trench looks like ruin, but it is the only way to clear space for the load-bearing pillars of your true destiny.

The PIT is the prescription because it is the only environment harsh enough to break the heavily defended, stubborn self we build to protect our pride. In the daylight of success, we rely on our titles, intellect, and our coping mechanisms to keep up appearances, completely unaware that our internal framework is rotting. But when the walls cave in and resources drop to zero, those superficial defenses collapse.

The PIT strips away your illusions of control until your soul finally becomes soft, pliable, and ready for alignment. It is precisely in this low, unyielding dirt that you are made ready to receive the blueprints of a divine choreography the patient, precise rearrangement of your life by a goodness that has never forgotten you.

Reflection Questions:

What if the place I have been trying hardest to escape is actually the place where the deepest work within me is meant to begin?

What parts of my identity, pride, expectations, or false sources of security are being exposed or dismantled by this season that could not have been revealed any other way?

If the PIT is an excavation rather than a punishment, what unstable foundations in my life is God preparing to remove before something stronger can be built?

What am I clinging to that prevents me from surrendering to the possibility that my greatest transformation may require letting go before I can move forward?

Chapter One

Navigating the Darkest Place

A Journey to Light

The beauty of life can be difficult to recognize when darkness surrounds you, draining your spirit and weakening your desire to live. Yet, in such moments, something remarkable emerges: an inner cry out to God which starts the process of cleansing the soul, allowing genuine healing to take hold. A healing process rooted in spiritual alignment, reconnecting, and restoring your inner self.

The Descent into Darkness

The descent into deep darkness seldom arrives with warning. It starts subtly yet suddenly, as if an internal brightness is being turned down; the vibrancy and vitality of life slowly loses its intensity. Finally with the light fading all at once.

This darkness is not simply the absence of happiness. It is something more palpable than a heavy presence that settles over the soul. It silences hope, distorts memory, and makes even familiar things feel strange. Sometimes whispering doubts, you didn't choose, while amplifying fears you thought you'd outgrown. It wraps even your most cherished memories in a layer of grief, as if to remind you of everything you've lost.

At the center of this darkness lives what I call "pain." Pain not the ordinary ache of a hard day, but a deep, searing suffering that lives in the body and disorients the mind. It is the tightness in the chest that never fully let's go. It is anxiety that coils tighter with each passing hour. It carries with it a terrible sense of permanence, as though this is simply how things are now, and how they will always be.

Alongside the pain comes uncertainty like a fog that erases landmarks previously relied on faltering purpose and direction. Even the sense of who you are. Clarity becomes a stranger. Questions multiply without answers. The future, once a horizon of possibility, becomes a distant gray wall.

Somewhere within all of this, there is often a specific turning point in a Place in Time (PIT). This is not one bad week. It is a sustained period where everything converges old wounds, new failures, mounting pressure, and perhaps a single shattering event that breaks something loose. The PIT is where the darkness feels most dark and real, where the idea of getting out feels almost impossible.

One of the cruelest features of the PIT is what it takes from you quietly is the appreciation for what remains. Joy becomes dull. Beauty goes unnoticed. Kindness from others can't seem to reach through the haze. This loss deepens the isolation, because the very things that might anchor us like connection, gratitude, and wonder become inaccessible. One drifts further from the shore. Time slips away, turning days into weeks and months into nothingness.

If you are in this place right now, please hear this: the PIT is real, but it is not the whole story. It is a chapter in your life, not the ending.

When Darkness Becomes Physical

The darkness we carry inside our mind does not stay inside. It moves into the body dictating how we eat, sleep, and sometimes hold ourselves beyond the reach for others.

Appetite is often one of the first things to shift. Some people stop eating because food loses its taste, affecting the body's will to nourish. While some eat compulsively, searching for the only place that still offers any comfort. Neither is a moral failure. Both are the body's honest attempt to cope with a distinct pain it wasn't built to carry.

Intimacy becomes difficult, too. Not just physical closeness, but the vulnerability of truly being seen and understood. When you are in survival mode, connection takes energy simply don't have. You may find yourself retreating not because you don't want to be loved, but because the armor required to function leaves little room for warmth compounding the pain because of isolation. It is not permanent.

Engaging in physical activity exercise and simply going outside can feel like an insurmountable challenge. The body grows sluggish, mirroring the stagnation of the spirit. This is not laziness but the result of the weight of what you're carrying. In time, the body signals its own desire to heal. A craving for cleaner food. An intuitive pull toward fresh air. A small, but persistent voice that says: I want to feel better.

Listening to that voice matters.

There is a Japanese practice called Shinrin-yoku a kind of forest bathing which is the simple act of being present in nature. Not hiking aggressively, not achieving anything. Just being among trees, or by water, or under an open sky. Research consistently shows that this kind of contact with the natural world lowers stress, calms the nervous system, and restores a sense of proportion to problems that feel enormous indoors. Nature has a way of reminding us that we are part of something much larger than our current suffering and very therapeutic.

Self-care during dark times is not an indulgence but a necessity. Drinking water. Sleeping when you can. Taking slow walks. These are not small things; they are acts of self-compassion, signaling that you still believe in yourself. One day in the future you may reflect on this time not as pain but as promise.

Battling the Inner Landscape

The mind in darkness is a difficult place to live. It becomes a territory of distortion where fear and uncertainty outsizes every memory confirming the worst by casting a bleak future. Navigating this inner landscape requires both honesty and gentleness.

Fear is one of the most relentless residents of this territory, and it does not always reveal itself as fear. Sometimes it masquerades as certainty that you'll never get better. Echoing, I am fundamentally broken, and things will always be this way. Some of these thoughts feel like facts. They are not. They are the product of a mind under extreme stress, doing its best to make sense of pain it doesn't know how to process.

Loneliness in darkness is also particularly cruel, because it persists even when you are surrounded by other people. Feelings of being fundamentally misunderstood, watching others live with ease can sometimes feel foreign while convincing that engagement is pointless. Making connections, even an imperfect connection, is one of the most powerful counterforces to despair. One honest conversation can shift something and give you a new outlook and life trajectory.

Perceptions can become unreliable because the mind gravitates towards a negative framework which filters out evidence of hope and magnifies evidence of hopelessness. It is not lying to you maliciously it is doing what a threatened mind does. Recognizing this distortion as a low hanging fruit is the first step toward addressing something important to our mood and emotional well-being.

Meditation, particularly simple mindfulness practices, can help create a small but meaningful gap between you and your thoughts. This practice doesn't eliminate the pain but allows you to observe it objectively without being entirely consumed by it. Even five minutes of intentional stillness can interrupt the rumination loop enough to offer a breath of relief and the ability to objectively access your mindset.

Journaling is another underrated tool. When thoughts spiral endlessly in the mind, giving them a place to land on a page, a screen, any external surface can bring a sense of order and reflection. Patterns become visible. The rumination loops slow down, and you begin to see your own thinking rather than simply being a reactive participant. Journaling has helped me tremendously by contributing to my mental health journey while documenting my spiritual growth.

Those who find meaning and understanding in spiritual practices like prayer, scripture, worship, and quiet reflection can produce a spiritual grounding effect. This grounding for many people can be an opportune way for developing a deeper understanding of all things spiritual.

Spiritual Reconnection

Darkness does profound damage to the spirit. It severs the threads that connect us to ourselves, to others, and to whatever we understand as sacred or transcendent. The spirit, a resilient force, continues to reach for Divine connection despite the damage.

One of the earliest losses is the desire to wonder. The world that once felt alive with meaning with small miracles and beauty hiding in ordinary moments somehow goes black. Questions that once sparked something in you become apathetic. The sacred seems distant because of the perception of unanswered questions. This is a real loss, and it deserves to be named as one because sometimes we already know the answer.

There is also a kind of inner disconnection which is a sense of being estranged not just from others, but from yourself. Your own voice sounds muffled. Your instincts feel unreliable. You are present in your life but perceiving the world as somehow unreal or distorted. In extreme cases, this can tip into dissociation a strange, unsettling sense of watching yourself from the outside.

In the search for reconnection, ancient practices still hold power. Prayer as a necessity of communicating in an unguarded and supernatural way.

Fasting provides spiritual clarity because it demonstrates that we are ready for something deeper to surface.

What the spirit is ultimately seeking, beneath all the striving and the pain is the comfort in which God can only give. The longing we experience is a connection with God. Meditation provides the combination of stillness and openness to quiet the mind and to open the heart in a particularly powerful way. Together, they create conditions for a peaceful mind that is not simply the absence of pain, but something more in harmony that comes from being spiritually aligned.

The Journey of Transformation

No one transforms alone. The path through darkness is rarely a solo journey, even when it feels that way. Understanding the landscape and what the darkness is, why it arrived, and where it might lead is the work you'll come to understand in the preceding chapters.

Personal stories matter immensely. When someone who has walked through darkness shares their experience honestly, not cleaned up something shifts in the listener. The isolation breaks. A rational thought appears: if they survived this, perhaps I can too.

Professional support is a wise choice, too. A good therapist, counselor, or psychiatrist offers something that love from family and friends cannot always provide: a trained perspective, a safe container, and specific tools for working through what has accumulated. Typical talk therapy tools include cognitive behavior therapy which is recommended. Asking for that kind of help is one of the most honest things a person in pain can do.

Understanding why the darkness arrived matters. Rather than assigning blame to yourself or anyone else, try giving the suffering a shape, context, and a reason. Trauma, loss, chronic stress, spiritual crisis, and neurological factors do not exist in isolation. Understanding them can loosen the grip of shame and point toward the right kind of healing. Recovery moves in increments.

Some days might feel like enormous progress while others feel like falling backward. The key is not to measure yourself against a straight upward line, but to notice, over time, whether you are feeling better, maintaining a peaceable mindset and taking care of your mind, body, and spirit. A sign of transformation is the gradual return of gratitude noticing what's still good. Enjoying a meal, laughing, recognizing the sky's color, or hearing birds chirp are small yet meaningful signs that darkness is fading.

The Source of Light and Strength

When everything else has been stripped away revealing why self-reliance has run out, coping strategies have been exhausted, exposes a mind which is too exhausted to argue itself into hope becomes an opportunity for a spiritual encounter. Many people find themselves turning toward something they can't fully explain.

Call it God, the Divine, the sacred, the universe, or a higher power. The name matters less than the orientation, which is the willingness to look beyond yourself for what you cannot grapple alone. This kind of guidance often arrives quietly. Through a passage in a book that lands at exactly the right moment. Through the unexpected counsel of someone who seems to say precisely what was needed. Through prayer that begins as a desperate outpouring and ends not with an answer, but with a strange, sense of being comforted. This is a good place to be because it builds spiritual capacity.

The PIT, for all its anguish, can function as a kind of spiritual incubator. In the same way that a seed must break through the darkness of the soil before it can reach the light, the breaking-open that happens in our deepest struggles can release something that could not have emerged in any other way. Resilience, depth, and compassion are born not from theory but from having genuinely suffered. These are not small gifts; they come at an enormous cost.

There is also something important in the relationship between faith in something larger than yourself and belief in yourself. They are not separate. When you understand yourself as having been made with purpose and responsible for carrying something unique and irreplaceable during the dark times, it becomes sustainable.

Surrender, in this context, is not giving up. It is releasing the exhausting belief that you must control everything alone. It is trusting that even when you cannot see the path, something is still guiding. That the darkness, however real, does not have the final word.

Your responsibility is to open your heart and mind to receive divine instruction as spiritual guidance. God understands where we falter and as is patient with our performance, consistency, and ability to hold ourselves together. This guidance is available, especially when we need it the most. For many people living in the PIT, this is the single most radical and transformative experience they'll ever encounter because it's sustaining and aligns with their purpose.

Loving yourself with care is just important, not as an aspiration but as a practice. It means accepting what the darkness revealed about you without letting it define you. It means forgiving yourself for whatever choices brought you there. Also, for the ways you may have hurt yourself or others while you were lost and broken. It means recognizing that you are not a finished project, but a living one. It also means doing what is necessary to get better by seeking help when you need it even when it feels impossible.

The darkness will change you. It was always going to. The question now is whether you will let it make you smaller, or whether you will carry what you'll learn into something larger than you could have been before.

The light is not behind you. It is in front of you.

CHAPTER TWO

The Crucible of Now

Transforming Time in Place

The Destination

There is a particular kind of suffering that cannot be outran. No matter how many times a person tries to escape by changing their surroundings by ending relationships, or making a fresh start, the pain you are fleeing often arrives before you do. This suffering is not rooted in external circumstances or physical location. It is an internal state, a condition that follows you until you are willing to face it directly. Only when one stops running and acknowledges its presence does the possibility for true transformation truly begin.

There comes a moment in the journey through suffering when the impulse to flee finally falters. This chapter is about what happens when you stop running. When every attempt to escape by changing your environment, relationships, or circumstances proves futile until resistance eventually loses its strength. It is in this space, when resistance exhausts itself, that another process begins to take shape.

This new beginning is not quick or easy. It is slower, more challenging, and requires a deeper kind of strength than running ever did. The transformation that unfolds here is not about immediate relief or dramatic change.

Instead, it is a gradual, powerful shift that emerges only when you are willing to face your pain directly, to stop fighting what is, and to engage with the reality of your experience. This is one of the most important lessons in life.

It is precisely in this surrender when the effort to escape is spent, and you remain present with your suffering that true healing finds room to grow. This is the threshold where endurance, understanding, and, ultimately, transformation becomes possible.

The word "crucible" is precise here. A crucible is not a comfortable place. It is a vessel designed for extreme heat, used to burn away everything that doesn't belong. What emerges is not unchanged; it is purified. Stronger at the broken places more than it was before. I have vivid memories of working in the laboratory at Acme Steel in Riverdale, Illinois where we made steel ingots for the automobile industry. I worked in quality assurance and used a spectrometer to test hot molten ingot samples for the correct metallurgy.

In a foundry, a crucible is a high-temperature container specifically designed to melt, hold, or transfer molten metal for casting processes. It is a critical component in metal melting operations, where it must withstand extreme heat, thermal shock, and chemical exposure. The Place in Time (PIT) functions this way. What feels like confinement is also incubation. What feels like destruction is also formation. The transformation available inside the PIT is not something that happens despite its difficulty; rather, it is fundamentally intertwined with that very difficulty. The struggle, the sense of confinement, and the enduring pain are not obstacles to change but are the very conditions through which growth is forged.

Just as a crucible uses intense heat to refine and purify, the PIT functions as an environment where the hardest experiences become the source of new strength, clarity, and depth. What feels destructive is also formative, creating the possibility for resilience and compassion that could not be realized in any other way. The darkness does not merely precede the transformation it is how it becomes possible.

Transforming Time in Place

The destination is what I've come to call the Time in Place (TIP): not an escape from your circumstances, but a dynamic, active engagement with them. A space where you discover the power to forge a new direction, not around your suffering, but through it. The PIT is where you begin, and the TIP is the ending phase.

The TIP represents a fundamental shift in perspective. Rather than seeking relief through avoidance or withdrawal, it encourages you to remain present with your situation. This presence is not passive; it is a deliberate, ongoing interaction with your reality. The pain and discomfort are not sidestepped or minimized but acknowledged and addressed with intentionality.

Within the TIP, you begin to recognize that true transformation does not result from circumventing hardship. Instead, it emerges from moving directly through the experience, allowing the difficulties to shape and refine you. As you actively engage with your circumstances, you find strength and clarity that would not have been possible through escape. This approach transforms suffering into an opportunity for growth, revealing new pathways and possibilities that were previously hidden within the struggle.

The TIP is not defined by the absence of pain, but by the presence of purpose and agency. It is an invitation to participate fully in your own healing and growth, forging a new direction that honors both the reality of your suffering and the potential for renewal that lies within it. The first response to the PIT is almost always resistance. Anything that might dissolve the walls of the confinement and return us to the life we recognize is a deeply human response and ultimately, futile.

The harder you press against the walls of the PIT, the more energy you spend which could be directed toward understanding, navigating, and eventually transcending the very circumstances you're fighting. Resistance does not shorten the sentence. It often lengthens it. As the futility of escape becomes apparent, the emotional weight intensifies. Depression deepens. Pain that has been suppressed resurfaces with unexpected force.

Spiritual Disconnection

In the deepest depths of the PIT brings a profound sense of hollowness. A feeling of being untethered and severed from anything transcendent. This sensation seeps into every aspect of your existence, manifesting not just as emotional distress but as physical symptoms that defy clear medical explanation. Sleep becomes disrupted, energy collapses, and the body appears to carry the weight of invisible burdens. In this state, the boundaries that separate emotional, spiritual, and physical suffering dissolve, leaving you enveloped in complete and undifferentiated pain.

As desperation mounts, there is often a turn toward external fixes in hopes of relief. Medication may dull the sharpest edges, but it cannot reach the core of the suffering. Distractions fill the hours, offering temporary reprieve, yet they fail to address the underlying wound. The quick solutions are those most readily grasped in moments of distress and merely skim the surface and leave the deeper pain untouched.

This period of suffering feels like spiritual demolition. The foundations of faith, once steady and secure, begin to erode. The inner peace that previously acted as a sanctuary is shattered, and a sense of drifting replaces hope. In this darkness, envisioning a way out feels impossible. Yet, what remains unseen in the midst of this demolition is its essential role: it is the precondition for reconstruction. The breaking down of old certainties and comforts creates space for something new to be built within the darkness itself.

When you stop fighting your circumstances, seeking external escapes, or new relationships; they only deepen the spiritual prison because it's superficial. The real work is not out there. It is in here.

The PIT is not a form of punishment. It is a passage and like all meaningful passages, it has terrain you must traverse, stages you must move through, a process that cannot be skipped without cost.

Much like metal placed into a crucible and exposed to extreme heat, the spirit within the PIT is subjected to rigorous testing and refinement. This intense process does not destroy the essence of who you are; rather, it serves to burn away false certainties and brittle defenses which were never truly part of your authentic self.

What is removed in this fiery ordeal is not a realistic loss, but instead a profound act of clarification. The unnecessary layers and the illusions you once relied upon are stripped away, revealing a core that is clearer, stronger, and more aligned with your true identity. Through this process, the suffering endured in the PIT becomes a catalyst for discovering who you are becoming, unburdened by the things that no longer serve you.

Within the crucible, a pivot point arrives. It is not dramatic. It is simply a deeply personal and quiet moment when you decide to stop resisting the pain and begin engaging with it.

The Power of Choice

Choosing to heal is not an act that eliminates suffering. Instead, it initiates a profound shift in how you relate to your pain. Where agony was once seen solely as an adversary, it now takes on the role of a teacher. The difficulties that previously felt empty or pointless begin to reveal their significance. They direct attention toward wounds in need of care, highlight patterns requiring change, and encourage a more honest understanding of oneself.

This decision marks the beginning of a different journey. It does not promise immediate or total change, but it sets you on a path where transformation is possible. The choice to heal reshapes everything, gradually, and in the ways that matter most. For many who find themselves traversing the PIT, confronting the question of God becomes unavoidable. Often, the first instinct is to bargain, to reason, or to demand that the suffering be explained, justified, or at least shortened. When these demands are met with silence, the crisis can deepen, intensifying feelings of isolation and uncertainty.

Yet, for those who are willing to continue moving forward, a subtle but profound shift occurs. The urgency for immediate answers gradually loosens its grip. In its place, a more patient form of faith begins to take root, not the faith grounded in easy certainty, but the challenging faith that trusts in a wisdom greater than what we can comprehend. The willingness to say, "I do not know why this is happening, but I trust the process; I trust the One who holds the process," marks a significant turning point.

The journey transforms from one demanding an explanation to one cultivating trust, and this shift is among the most consequential changes that can occur during the passage through the PIT.

Mindset Shift and Emergence

After enduring the crucible's demanding cycle of reflection, decision-making, and persistence, the journey starts to change in subtle ways. This change is not sudden or dramatic; rather, it unfolds slowly and quietly. At first, the transformation may go unnoticed, as the overwhelming negativity that once dominated every moment starts to diminish.

With time, clarity emerges in brief, unexpected moments. These glimpses of understanding signal the loosening of the PIT's grip. While the release is not absolute or immediate, it is significant enough to mark a turning point. The persistent heaviness that defined the experience gradually recedes, allowing space for new perspectives and renewed hope to take root. This is the ascent.

As the journey through the PIT progresses, the pain endured and the difficulties faced begin to blend into something more meaningful, a form of wisdom. These experiences, though never sought out, gradually reveal themselves as having served a purpose. It may not feel as though the hardships were deserved, but in time, it becomes clear that they have been used, transformed into something valuable.

The suffering does not remain pointless or wasted. Instead, it acts as a force that shapes and refines you. Through the trials and the endurance required to move forward, each challenge contributes to your growth, leaving you with a deeper understanding and a sense of clarity that could not have been gained in any other way. The wisdom that emerges is not theoretical; it is born from the lived reality of overcoming adversity, and it stands as evidence that the pain was not in vain.

In this stage, acceptance deepens and shifts from passive resignation to actively recognizing reality, encompassing past events, present situations, and personal limitations. This approach often brings a unique sense of freedom that can only be truly understood through direct experience. The effort once spent resisting is now channeled toward healing, opening avenues for growth and greater clarity.

A paradox may emerge here: the act of mentally and emotionally releasing the PIT not through denial, but through a willingness to stop being consumed by it can itself accelerate the healing. When you stop defining yourself primarily by your darkest chapter, a new chapter begins to form. This is not the abandonment of the truth. It is a refusal to let the truth of your suffering become your whole story.

What emerges on the far side of the ascent is not the person who entered the PIT, but a person has been transformed. You'll carry the marks of the journey not as wounds to hide, but as evidence of what you've endured demonstrating your spiritual capability. A clearer sense of purpose. A more honest understanding of your own values. A capacity for compassion, born not from theory but from having genuinely suffered, that no easier life could have produced. The ascent is not an escape from the PIT. It is an evolution born from its depths.

The Sanctuary and Crucible

The PIT was a horrible place until it became my sanctuary. I want to be honest about that before I say anything else. There was nothing initially redemptive about it, nothing that felt like growth while I was inside it. It was confinement. It was pain. It was the slow, grinding experience of a life that had stalled and a self that had fractured.

Gradually, my perspective shifted.

This was not because my suffering suddenly ceased, but because I started to realize that the pain itself carried a purpose. The PIT served as an incubator, nurturing qualities within me that could never have developed in the comfort of easier circumstances.

In this place of hardship, I found a crucible where intense heat stripped away everything I had previously mistaken for my true self. The arrogance that had once defined me, the sense of self-sufficiency I clung to, and the intricate defenses I constructed to avoid vulnerability, all began to melt away. The PIT demanded a kind of openness and honesty that I had long resisted, burning away those barriers and leaving only what was essential for healing. It was in this environment, where all pretense was stripped, where genuine transformation could begin.

Most of the time, honestly, it was still a mental prison. But I was learning something inside that prison that I could not have learned anywhere else, finally a door opened where I could find solace.

I learned to overcome myself. Not just the circumstances around me, but the patterns within me, the resistance, stubbornness, and the compulsive need to control. I learned to become attentive to the quiet directions that came through prayer and the small inklings when followed, led somewhere meaningful. I was being readied for God.

For several years, I attended church regularly and grew in ways I hadn't expected not just in knowledge, but in wisdom, which was something different. Wisdom is knowledge that has been tested. Earned. You can't acquire it by reading about it. You have to live it.

The desire to escape was always present. I won't pretend otherwise. But I knew, somewhere beneath the restlessness, that turning my back on the process a second time would cost me more than staying. I had already experienced how to live in a chaotic world without a spiritual anchor, and I did not want to go back to that.

The Pathway to Healing

I began volunteering at Sacramento's Loaves and Fish, a local food shelter dedicated to serving the homeless population. Each time I helped, I felt a deep sense of gratitude for the opportunity to support others, especially those facing greater hardships than my own.

These moments of service were not one-sided; often, I found myself on the receiving end of wisdom, as many individuals I served shared their life journeys with me. Their stories provided perspective and, at times, unexpected guidance.

Calvary Christian Center became my home away from home. I invested both my time and energy in the construction of the new church building, finding purpose in contributing to something lasting and meaningful. On weekends, our church hosted "Church on the Street" events at a local park.

During these gatherings, we prepared food and offered prayers for people in need, creating a space of care and spiritual support within the community. Additionally, I volunteered with the Sacramento Medical Foundation's African American Bone Marrow Committee. This important work of speaking directly to the community about the bone marrow registry added another layer of meaning to my journey, allowing me to contribute to important causes beyond my immediate church and neighborhood. Through these acts of service, I not only aided others but also created a new dimension of healing within myself.

The Air Force taught me the importance of volunteering and servicing others. Serving others was a natural form of healing and gave me the ability to distance myself temporarily from my own pain. It was not a cure. I was still hurting. But it gave me a reason to show up, and showing up is which I still do today.

Over time, I began to see something essential that changed my entire perspective. The true cause of my pain was not the broken relationship itself. Though it was the event that cracked open my defenses, what spilled forth had existed long before her presence in my life. The pain had its roots in my own separation from God, shaped by spiritual barriers I had erected sometimes knowingly and sometimes unconsciously to keep transformation under control and at a distance.

Releasing emotional residue from that relationship became one of the most difficult tasks I have ever faced. It was not because the person was irreplaceable, but rather because I had allowed grief to become part of my identity. Holding onto the pain kept me anchored in a familiar narrative, while letting go meant stepping into the uncertainty of discovering who I might truly become.

The breakthrough did not arrive in a burst of inspiration, but in a moment of honest confrontation. I looked directly at my resistance, stubbornness, and desire for control and made the choice to stop defending them. I recognized that many of the challenges I faced, and my repeated inability to move forward, stemmed in large part from my own belief, decision, and perspective. This acknowledgment was not about self-condemnation; it was about accepting accountability. The path ahead became clear only when I stopped blaming external obstacles and began to examine the one person who constantly encountered them: myself.

When I finally understood that I was the architect of the barriers by blocking my own healing and that I possessed the power to dismantle them, everything began to shift. This change did not happen instantly, but it altered my direction. And with sustained commitment, direction ultimately determines destination.

The crucible is not a comfortable place to live. It is a space marked by discomfort and challenge, where familiar comforts are stripped away, and the realities of one's inner world are laid bare. Yet, for those who are willing to remain in this place long enough, it becomes one of the most transformative places a human being can inhabit. Enduring the present with openness and patience allows for growth that cannot occur elsewhere.

The PIT does not ask for your permission. It does not wait for you to feel ready or invite you in gently. Instead, it demands your presence with your honest, sustained, and undefended presence. The process asks only that you show up as you are, relinquishing pretense and allowing yourself to be seen, even if only by yourself. By granting the PIT this kind of presence, you open the door to discovering what you are truly made of. In meeting this experience with sincerity and endurance, you uncover inner resources, resilience, and strength that might have otherwise remained hidden. Consistently and authentically showing up is what enables transformation to take root.

The PIT is not the end of your story.
It is where your real story begins.

CHAPTER THREE

The Open Door

The Invitation to the Next Chapter

The Path to Readiness

Within the PIT, there exists a closed door which may go unnoticed, yet it remains present. When experiencing the deepest moments within the PIT, where darkness feels enduring and the walls are cold and unyielding, the door does not offer an apparent way of escape. It remains inconspicuous for those struggling.

Positioned in the dark shadows, the door awaits discovery not through effort, but rather when readiness arises. Within the depths of the PIT, the door feels distant and unreachable and at times invisible to those caught in the throes of struggle. The door remains closed until a particular readiness emerges within you. It is only when you have reached this state when you are prepared in heart and mind that the door opens, signaling a new chapter.

This pivotal moment is not simply a decision you make; it is often a surrender shaped by the entirety of your journey up to this point. The many paths that have led you here, though different in their details, share a common thread.

Only those who arrive at this threshold truly understand the cost of persistent pain, the exhaustion from ongoing internal battles, and the profound shift that takes place when the familiar self begins to give way to something unknown. It is the culmination of endurance, struggle, and acceptance that allows the door to open, marking the transition into a new phase of life.

The Work Begins

And this is where the most important work of your life begins. Many who find themselves in this space come to realize, sometimes reluctantly, a deeper reliance on something spiritual and divinely greater than their own willpower.

The understanding that we cannot control the world, other people, or even our own thoughts may arrive as an epiphany, but it is a crucial step toward the open doorway. The pain of the past, though persistent, remains a part of your story and not a judgment on your worth. What you choose to do at this moment is what carries forward into the next chapter of your life.

Entering this new inner environment can bring with it a sense of volatility and unpredictability. Emotions that previously felt manageable can surge unexpectedly, creating a landscape marked by destitution, disconnection, confusion, and fear.

The strategies once relied upon to manage feelings become ineffective, and the anxiety of the unknown can grip your body with overwhelming force. Grief, no longer held in check, often expresses itself as uncontrollable weeping. Anger may erupt suddenly or simmer quietly beneath the surface.

Even the simplest daily tasks can feel insurmountable, adding to the sense of disorientation and challenge. It is important to recognize that these reactions are not signs of weakness. Rather, they represent the honest and visceral response of someone whose inner foundations have shifted. The upheaval is part of the process, a reflection of transformation at work.

To survive in this emotionally turbulent space requires an approach that may feel counterintuitive: instead of fighting against your feelings, allow yourself to experience them fully. Acknowledging and giving space to emotions whether grief, fear, or anger is not surrendering to weakness or self-indulgence; it is an act of wisdom.

When grief is allowed to move through you, it loses its power to immobilize. Naming your fear enables you to examine it with clarity. Expressing anger honestly and nonviolently prevents it from causing unseen harm. Through this practice of acceptance and presence, you begin to transform your inner landscape not by force, but with authenticity and patience while processing your emotions.

The journey from emotional chaos to a new kind of balance is not achieved by pushing through or ignoring what is real. Instead, it demands patience, self-compassion, and a particular kind of courage to remain present with your true feelings and experiences. This willingness to stay with what is real, rather than escaping or suppressing it, allows for growth and healing.

Your journey to this point, however circuitous, has been more than a crucible. Seasons spent searching, the persistence of your deepest questions, and moments of grace you never expected have all played a role in shaping who you are now. You have not arrived here broken beyond repair; rather, you are the result of everything you have endured and learned.

You carry with you more strength, wisdom, and experience than you may realize.

Now, you stand at this threshold bearing the full weight of your own story. A tapestry woven from life's lessons, subtle spiritual insights, failures that became teachers, relationships that required sacrifice, and silences that spoke volumes. This moment is not simply a mental or emotional state; it is a true turning point.

At this juncture, the invitation as unusual as it may seem is to pause and allow yourself to be present in the moment of reflection. Settle into the present. Resist the immediate impulse to fix or solve everything. Instead, reflect not only on what might await you beyond this door, but also on what is happening within you as you stand at its threshold.

Stepping Through the Open Door

Stepping through that open door marks a pivotal moment, one that calls for immediate introspection and a gentle, honest assessment of both heart and mind. Rather than clinging to old patterns of resistance, the focus shifts toward cultivating a quiet ease, especially in the face of uncertainty.

The familiar question, "now what?" evolves from a cry of confusion into a patient inquiry grounded in the acceptance of what is, reflecting an openness to whatever may unfold next. It is important to recognize that this approach is not synonymous with giving up. Instead, it reflects the process of learning to inhabit the present moment fully, without trying to force it into a shape it is not yet ready to take.

By allowing yourself to be present with what is, you create space for clarity and growth, trusting that answers and direction will come in their own time.

My journey across the threshold began with a single, unwavering decision: to wait. This meant placing my trust in a healing process that was neither within my control nor fully visible to me. I made the choice to embrace uncertainty, believing that something meaningful could emerge from patience and surrender. I wanted to hear from God and I was ready to come closer.

Transformation Over Medication

In my search for answers regarding my life path, I was faced with a decision to reject prescription medication for something I knew was based my spiritual condition. My conviction at the time was that what I needed most was not chemical relief, but the slower, more demanding work of spiritual transformation. It is important to clarify that this decision was deeply personal and not a recommendation for others.

Each individual's journey through darkness is unique, and professional medical support is often not only wise but essential. For me, this choice was right in that moment, and I hold no regrets for having made it.

As I ventured deeper into the hidden recesses of my mind, I encountered challenges far greater than I had anticipated. The path was both difficult and demanding, yet the struggle itself became a source of unexpected gratitude. Through navigating these hardships, I uncovered strengths and insights that might have otherwise remained hidden.

In those early years, I was emotionally volatile with a fragile core shielded by a hard, arrogant exterior. My days were consumed by sorrow, grief, and uncontrollable anger. I believed that what I needed was greater willpower to overcome these challenges. Yet, in truth, what I truly craved was just peace of mind.

The sense of peace I sought rarely arrived in full or lasting form. Instead, it appeared only in fragments that sometimes lasted a few hours before the familiar darkness would return. These brief intervals of calm were never enough to permanently dispel the anguish, and inevitably, I found myself on my knees once again, pleading for relief.

This was the pattern that defined my experience for the first three years: a relentless cycle, with no shortcuts or easy escape. The only option available was a daily commitment and a decision, renewed each day, to keep moving forward, despite the pain and uncertainty.

Stepping through that open door is not merely an act of moving ahead; it is a journey that demands sincere and ongoing introspection. At times, the temptation to rely exclusively on your own strength may feel overpowering, yet this approach often results in repeated frustration. It is important to understand that such frustration is not a reflection of personal inadequacy. Rather, it arises from the nature of the healing that is required in this season of life.

This kind of healing cannot be achieved by force or sheer determination. Willpower alone is insufficient. Instead, true growth and transformation must be cultivated with patience and gentleness, allowing space for these changes to unfold naturally. By nurturing this process, you create an environment in which healing can emerge in its own time, rather than attempting to rush it or shape it prematurely.

The Power of Honest Expression

Crying out to God should not be viewed as a sign of defeat; instead, it represents a vital and cathartic act of release. Relinquishing the constant need to appear strong and allowing ourselves to be truly heard even if that audience is simply our own unguarded hearts causes something within to shift. The sincere expression of pain, fear, or grief opens the door to transformation, a change that cannot occur when we are focused on performing strength or avoiding vulnerability.

In this space of honesty, we discover the possibility of connection, renewal, and the first steps toward healing.

During periods of adversity, the support and spiritual guidance offered by others become essential resources. Through prayer, companionship, or simple gestures, these connections supply comfort and strength often unavailable when facing difficulties alone. Appropriately timed words or actions are capable of alleviating barriers to connection, providing hope and reassurance. Although not easily quantified, this support has a substantial impact.

The shared experience of faith or empathy extends into personal challenges, reinforcing the importance of communal engagement in the healing process. True inner growth is rooted in the process of purification. While the term may sound severe, in practice, purification is simply the act of clearing out.

This process begins with mental purification, which requires intentional introspection. By looking closely at the narratives we create and carry within ourselves, we can discern which stories continue to serve us and which are ready to be released. This honest self-examination allows us to let go of those inner narratives that no longer support our well-being, making space for new understanding and growth.

In contrast, spiritual purification is cultivated through dedicated practices such as prayer, meditation, and silence. These gentle disciplines guide us toward a deeper spiritual connection with ourselves and God. Through them, we learn to move beyond the layers of armor and anxiety that accumulate over time, gradually uncovering a more authentic alignment with who we are at our core.

In this space, growth and transformation are allowed to unfold naturally, without force or haste. This work is slow, requiring patience and perseverance. Yet, it stands as the most important work there is, laying the foundation for lasting inner change and the possibility of true transformation.

What I eventually understood was that I had no control over my thoughts or emotions. I realized I had been using past pain as an excuse for self-pity, avoiding the fact that much of my suffering was self-inflicted.

Writing this is difficult; living it was even harder.

It took years before I found a peaceful mindset not through sheer willpower, but by consistently renewing my mind through prayer, meditation, and scripture. This daily practice helped me focus on healing rather than lingering on old wounds, allowing me to move forward closer to the door.

I discovered that there was a unique liberation in letting go of managing my expectations and the urge to control every outcome. This realization came as I surrendered the need to orchestrate each step, recognizing that my role was not to force doors open, but to patiently wait for God's guidance and timing.

The act of surrender was not a sign of weakness or defeat; rather, it marked the moment when I acknowledged the importance of trusting in something greater than myself. In surrendering not as a concession, but as an expression of profound trust, I discovered something transformative.

The door I needed to enter was finally open. My readiness was the only requirement for stepping through. The journey was not about finding the door, but about preparing myself to walk through it when the time was right.

The door opened when I was ready.

The PIT was a place of refinement. My healing began when I surrendered to the divine process. It is worth being honest about what the unprepared mind looks like, because most of us have lived in it for longer than we have been willing to admit.

The unprepared mind prays, but its prayers are ultimatums. It approaches God with a list of required outcomes and measures the quality of the relationship by whether those outcomes are delivered on schedule. The unprepared mind concludes that it has been abandoned, or that God is withholding, or that its faith is somehow insufficient when the silence persists, or when the circumstances refuse to change, and answer arrives in a form other than the one demanded.

The door remains closed to an unprepared mind.

The Unprepared Mind

The unprepared mind frequently participates in spiritual disciplines not from a place of sincere receptivity, but rather to gain favor or exert influence over the Divine.

Fasting, for example, is often undertaken with the expectation that it operates as a form of currency, something to be traded for blessings or favorable outcomes. Similarly, prayer may be viewed as a task to be accumulated, believing that sheer volume or fervor will ensure a response. Acts such as regular attendance at religious gatherings or service to others are sometimes regarded as items for a spiritual résumé, meticulously documented and presented as evidence of qualification or worthiness at the threshold of spiritual progress.

Although these practices hold intrinsic value and can contribute to spiritual growth, the unprepared mind mistakenly interprets them as definitive proof of readiness. Instead of fostering genuine openness and transformation, these disciplines are misapplied as mechanisms for validation or leverage, obscuring the true purpose of spiritual practice.

Readiness for spiritual transformation is not determined by how many religious activities one performs or by assembling a list of spiritual accomplishments in hopes of securing a particular outcome. Instead, real readiness is demonstrated by the condition of the heart itself. This means cultivating a spirit that is truly open, willing to listen, to perceive, understand, and to put into practice the guidance that is offered. It is in this posture of receptivity and humility that the path to deeper spiritual growth unfolds.

It is common for the unprepared mind to misinterpret periods of comfort as evidence of achievement or completion. In difficult circumstances, there may be moments when distress lessens perhaps because support networks have formed; helpful practices are now in place, or the daily challenges have become easier to manage. These instances undoubtedly provide authentic relief, offering a sense of respite and stability.

However, it is important to recognize that such relief does not mark the resolution of the challenge itself. Instead, these moments serve as preparation, laying out the groundwork for the true resolution that is yet to come. When comfort is mistaken for achievement, there is a tendency to seek out substitutes that merely alleviate discomfort without addressing its root cause. This search for temporary ease can lead to overlooking the deeper, necessary work that must still be done. The challenge remains present, even if its intensity has lessened, resulting in a state of readiness which has not yet been fully attained.

Pursuing solutions prematurely, before reaching the proper stage of readiness, often results in a return to the work that was left incomplete. This return may come with greater clarity, highlighting the importance of completing the process and addressing the underlying issues rather than settling for superficial relief.

The Other Side of the Door

What lies beyond the door? It's important to clarify what it isn't: it's not the solution to every problem. It doesn't instantly banish depression, grant perfect purpose, or usher in all the changes we've been hoping for. Nor is it a permanent state that requires no ongoing effort or choice.

What awaits is presence and a vivid, unmistakable, profoundly intimate experience of being with something that knows you wholly and accepts you without hesitation. During the soul's search throughout every stage of the PIT with pleading prayers, bargaining, and silent stretches when answers seemed absent somehow culminates in quietness.

Here, peace arrives not as a reward for enduring enough pain, but as the natural result of finally becoming receptive to what was always available. During this spiritual encounter, the mind undergoes a unique transformation. The ceaseless mental chatter gradually slows down, making room for a calming experience. The ever-present anxiety begins to lose its grip and significance.

This change isn't triggered by outside events, but by an inner adjustment. Mind, body, and spirit align with a spiritual reality that wraps around them with insight and understanding. The support found here surpasses what any human relationship can offer, bringing a profound sense of being cherished and understood.

This is the peace for which the PIT always prepared you, not the absence of difficulties, but the presence of God amid them. This encounter isn't an escape from humanity; instead, it reveals that fully embracing and surrendering the human condition uncovers something divine. This revelation has always been accessible to anyone who develops the capacity to become peaceful enough to see it. This spiritual encounter is not the reward at the end of the PIT. It is the discovery, made possible by the readiness cultivated within it.

The Daily Practice

In this journey, prayer is understood as more than a mere petition. While asking for what is needed has its place, prayer here is viewed as conversation genuinely unhurried, and honest dialogue with a divine presence. This kind of prayer does not require performance; it invites you to come as you truly are, without pretense. The door opens more readily to an honest and sincere heart than to one that is merely performing.

Meditation, defined here as the intentional practice of interior stillness, is the most direct preparation for the communion that lies beyond the threshold. The aim is not to empty the mind completely, but to cultivate a mind capable of true stillness is the essence of readiness. This practice, whether in the quiet of morning or evening, shapes the very condition the door requires. Even a brief, daily return to stillness begins to transform the inner environment, making the door to communion increasingly perceptible.

Practices such as fasting and the pursuit of intentional simplicity serve a similar purpose through different means. By voluntarily setting aside what typically fills our attention, we create room for what is most deeply needed.

These disciplines do not function as leverage or bargaining tools; rather, they are forms of preparation. They clear the interior space, turning the soil of the soul so that the seed of readiness can take root and grow.

Equally important is the company of fellowship with others who are also practicing readiness and cultivating a peaceable mindset. Their presence and support are a form of grace not to be underestimated. We are not meant to approach this door entirely alone.

When our own resources falter and the noise threatens to obscure the door, the courage and stillness of another can remind us that the door is still present, that it has always been there, and that our practice is bearing fruit, even if we cannot always perceive it.

The door leads to the most significant encounter available to a human life which is the direct, interior, living communion with the God who placed you in this life at a particular time in history for a specific purpose.

The door does not open because you have suffered enough, or prayed enough, or performed sufficient spiritual discipline. It opens because you have become, in the deepest and most honest sense of the word, ready.

Ready to stop fighting what you cannot control. Ready to release the outcomes you have been gripping. Ready to receive what has been waiting to be given not as a reward, but as the natural consequence of a mind that has finally become still enough to recognize the gift.

The peace on the other side of that door is not earned. But the readiness to receive it must be cultivated. That cultivation is the work of the PIT. And the PIT, which seemed at the beginning like a prison with no exit, reveals itself peaceable enough to see clearly the door was always open waiting for you to become ready to walk through it.

Readiness is the key and a peaceable mindset grants access.

Chapter Four

The Courageous Leap

Stepping into Divine Purpose

Time in Place

This chapter focuses on making the decision to grow spiritually. It delves into embracing your purpose, even when things seem uncertain, and you're lacking clear answers. It describes fear as a partner to courage rather than an enemy. It highlights how opportunities emerge instead of waiting for fear to disappear.

The path from the PIT to Time in Place (TIP) moving from feeling trapped to living with purpose is, at its core, a journey defined by courage. This isn't courage fueled by certainty, but by dedication. Taking courageous steps is about being consistent and choosing your direction until it becomes your identity.

Courage goes beyond just physical bravery; it includes an intangible quality that becomes clear when witnessed. This involves tapping into resources outside of pure willpower, often found when individual resolve runs out. Many cultures suggest these moments are marked by a sense of divine surrender, not as failure, but as recognition of our human limitations. This type of courage moves past self-reliance, uncovering hidden strengths.

The deepest form of spiritual courage is shown when we accept uncertainty, act without certainty of success, and trust in a process whose results are unknown. This kind of faith isn't about never doubting; it's about continuing forward even when doubt is present.

Courage is often quieter and more persistent than we expect. It shows up when we choose to face difficult moments instead of avoiding them, and when we let go of what's familiar to embrace uncertainty and growth. True courage isn't about dramatic gestures; it's about staying engaged through discomfort and trusting new possibilities.

Ultimately, courage is found in the moment you choose, one more time, to trust rather than to retreat. It is the continual act of moving forward, even when doubt and fear are present, relying on the process and the readiness cultivated within.

God requires you to be courageous.

Not the courage of comfortable belief or the kind that costs nothing nor changes anything. Not the courage of agreeing, in principle, that faith is important while keeping the life you have built carefully arranged around its own safety. God requires courageous action that moves us in a guided direction. The courage that steps forward before the ground is certain. The courage that is willing to lose what it has achieved in order to align with our spiritual purpose.

This is not an invitation. It is a calling. And callings do not wait indefinitely for us to become comfortable enough to answer them.

The journey from the PIT to the TIP represents confinement to purpose at its core, a journey defined by this kind of courage. Not courage fueled by certainty, because certainty is rarely available at the threshold of genuine transformation. But courage fueled by dedication: the daily, sustained, costly commitment to keep moving in the direction of your purpose even when the path is not fully lit, even when the outcome is not guaranteed, even when everything you value is at stake.

This chapter explores three dimensions of courage. First: that God does not simply permit courage in your faith it's a requirement. Second: that the unknown is not an obstacle to your purpose but the very territory through which it must be walked. Third: that the deepest form of courage is sacrificial and the willingness to lay down what you have been to become in exchange for what you are called to be.

Courageous Faith

There exists a form of faith characterized primarily by the recognition of God's existence, the acceptance of scriptural truth, and belief in the reality of divine purpose. While this type of faith has value, it remains insufficient on its own. Throughout sacred history, God has continually required greater commitment than mere acknowledgment or belief.

Consider what the Divine asks of those it calls. Not certainty which would require no faith. Not comfort that produces nothing that the spirit needs most. What God asks for, again and again, in the lives of those who are called forward, is the willingness to move before the full picture is revealed. To trust before the evidence is complete. To act on what has been given without waiting for what has not yet been disclosed. This is not recklessness.

It is the specific shape that mature faith is required to take. A faith that only moves when all conditions are favorable is not faith. It is a calculation. And God is not asking for your calculations. God is asking for your trust the same kind that is required in the PIT, refined through suffering, and is now being asked to carry you across the threshold into the life your purpose requires.

God does not call you to courage because the journey is safe. God calls you to courage because the journey requires it and because the courage itself is part of what you are being formed into.

What does courageous faith look like in practice? It looks like moving when the inner prompting is clear, even when the external circumstances offer no confirmation. It looks like releasing the outcomes you have been managing and trusting the One who holds them with a wisdom that exceeds your own. It looks like refusing to let fear have the final word, not because the fear is wrong to be present, but because faith has been given something larger to stand on than what fear projects.

God has not called you to a life of managed risk and careful preservation. God has called you to a life of courageous faith that moves mountains because the mover is more powerful than the mountain. Your responsibility is not to guarantee the outcome. Your responsibility is to have the courage to obey.

The unknown is where your purpose lives.

One of the most confusing aspects of spiritual life is that our instincts draw us toward what we already know. As human beings, we rely on patterns and routines; we naturally seek out what feels safe and predictable, often trying to plan our journey even before understanding where we want to go. While planning can be helpful, it's not necessary to fully grasp your life's purpose. Your spiritual purpose lies ahead of you and calls you into new areas you haven't yet explored.

The Unknown

The unknown isn't a void. Courage helps you see this, while fear can keep you from ever finding out. It's in the realm of the unknown that divine provision is most apparent, appearing when human efforts have been exhausted. Once you've reached the limits of your own resources and plans, you'll realize something that was always true but hidden by self-reliance: you were never navigating this journey on your own.

Throughout the scriptural record, every meaningful act connected to purpose unfolds not in places of certainty, but within the territory of the unknown. Divine instructions are given before destinations are named, calling individuals to move forward without a clear map. Provision arrives only after the steps of faith are taken, rarely in advance. The miraculous parting of waters happens precisely when the journey begins when your feet touch the water, not while waiting safely on the shore. This pattern is not a sign of divine cruelty, but evidence of intentional design.

The unknown is not a void absent of God; rather, it is the place where God's presence becomes most vivid. In this space, self-reliance is no longer an option, and dependence on divine guidance becomes essential. To move courageously into the unknown is not to stretch self-reliance to its limits; it is to embrace and trust the guidance.

This courage is marked by a willingness to step forward based on what has already been given, instead of waiting for further assurances. It is the movement of someone who, through suffering and formation, has learned that the ground can be trusted even when it cannot be seen. This kind of faith is shaped by experience, revealing that what is unseen is not unsafe when guided by purpose and trust.

The unknown is not the territory beyond God's reach. It is the territory where God's reach becomes the only thing you are standing on and where you discover, for the first time, that it is enough. The threshold between what is familiar and what is unknown is often crowded with internal obstacles.

Unresolved grievances and unforgiveness weigh heavily, anchoring you to your past at the very moment your purpose is calling you forward. These burdens can act as a drag, making it difficult to move beyond previous experiences and relationships.

Distorted thinking contributes to false beliefs that have accumulated over time about what you deserve, what is possible, and what God is actually willing to do in your life all shape your perception of the unknown. Before you even enter new territory, these beliefs can make it appear more threatening and less navigable than it is.

There are several interior forces that stand between you and the courageous step forward: the fear of change, the comfort of the familiar even if it limits you, and the subtle arrogance of self-sufficiency that prefers a manageable life over an obedient one. These forces are not your enemies; instead, they represent the unfinished business from your time in the PIT. They surface at the threshold because this is precisely the place where they must be addressed and resolved.

External obstacles such as the voices of those who cannot see what has been revealed, cultural forces that measure value by standards unrelated to your purpose, and the isolation which makes the step feel more solitary are real but secondary. It is the internal work that determines whether these external challenges can prevent you from moving forward. If your internal landscape has been genuinely prepared through the formation that comes from the PIT, you will find the external obstacles navigable. Without this preparation, even natural gifts or external resources may not be enough to overcome them.

Courage at the threshold does not mean waiting until every obstacle is eliminated before you act. Instead, it means stepping forward while those obstacles are still present. It is a deliberate, honest, and eyes-open choice to move toward the unknown, trusting that the act of moving itself will produce the growth and transformation that resistance cannot.

Losing Everything for Purpose

Purpose-driven courage is not about gaining. It is about giving up what you think is important to living a fulfilled life

Taking bold steps toward your true purpose means being truly willing to give up what you have now, who you are, and even how you see yourself, so you can grow into what's needed for your calling. This isn't just figurative, it's exactly what pursuing a real calling demands. You have to let go of living for safety, release any identity built on self-reliance, and set aside your own plans, trusting instead in a path that goes beyond your current understanding.

True sacrifice means giving up something deeply cherished, not simply going through the motions or surrendering things of little importance. It's the real letting go of what you value, what you have created, and what you rely on. This form of sacrifice sets true courage apart from simple boldness. While boldness acts without fear, courage moves forward despite fully understanding the cost involved.

What You Are Being Asked to Sacrifice

You are being asked to let go of the illusion of control and the belief that managing every variable guarantees your desired outcomes. The PIT has shown, sometimes harshly, that this control was always limited and dependent on uncontrollable forces. True courage comes from recognizing and releasing this illusion as an obstacle.

You are called to let go of the comfortable version of your faith to embrace one that agrees with Divine purpose but still puts personal safety first. God wants obedience, not just agreement, and following a true calling often means giving up the easy life you've known for one that is demanding yet meant for you.

You're also asked to release your attachment to the timing of an idea that your purpose should unfold according to your plan and pace. Divine purpose follows its own schedule and letting go of your own timeline demands courage as you surrender when, how, and in what form things happen.

Finally, you must sacrifice the need for approval from those who can't see what you've been shown. Not everyone who loves you will understand your decisions, and not every community can join you on this journey. This kind of courage can feel lonely and painful, but it means moving forward toward what God has revealed to you, even when those you care about aren't ready to follow.

Sacrificial courage is not the courage of someone who has nothing to lose. It is the courage of someone who has everything to lose and chooses the calling anyway because they have come to understand that what they would be preserving is not worth more than what they are being called to become.

The Clearing Created by Sacrifice

The sacrifice required by courageous purpose is not an arbitrary loss, nor is it the result of aimless surrender. Sacrifice serves a clear and essential function: it creates the space both within and around you that is necessary for the life of purpose to take root and flourish. When you release what is familiar, you are not being punished. Instead, you are being prepared. The act of letting go allows you to move beyond the comfortable version of yourself and embrace the calling that awaits. It is impossible to hold tightly to the familiar while also receiving what is being offered through your purpose. The hands that grip the known cannot be open to the new.

Therefore, release becomes an intentional preparation for arrival, not a punitive measure.

What is gained through sacrificial courage cannot be replaced by anything achieved through self-preservation. The person who has sacrificed the illusion for their purpose has willingly laid down what they value in obedience to their calling receives something unique and irreplaceable.

This is the authority that comes from being tested at the deepest level and choosing the calling over comfort. Such authority is not born of arrogance; it is the fruit of genuine surrender. It is what distinguishes the testimony of a life lived in courageous purpose, transforming it from an inspiring story into evidence. The authority gained through sacrifice makes the outcome of this journey not merely anecdotal, but proof of what is possible when courage and obedience shape a life.

Courage as a Daily Practice

Courageous faith, the willingness to walk into the unknown, and the sacrifice required by purpose are not static achievements. Rather, they are ongoing practices and habits that must be intentionally chosen and cultivated as required. This orientation toward courage must be renewed every morning, reaffirmed in moments of uncertainty, and sustained throughout times when courage does not appear dramatic but is simply persistent.

Fear will continue to exist alongside faith. Its presence does not indicate a failure of faith; instead, it is the honest reality of a finite being responding to an infinite calling. The purpose is not to eradicate fear but to refuse to let it dictate one's actions. Fear provides valuable information about what matters most, where the stakes are highest, and what is treasured enough to fear its loss. Allow fear to inform your decisions, but do not permit it to govern your life.

Inner peace is the essential foundation of courageous living, not its reward. A mind that is constantly agitated or driven by anxiety and urgency cannot discern the quiet voice of Divine direction with enough clarity to act faithfully. The cultivation of stillness through prayer, meditation, and honest self-reflection of what motivates your choices is not an escape from courageous living, but the necessary groundwork. Faithful action is only possible when there is clarity of guidance.

The decision to step forward must be made repeatedly. Courage is not a singular, dramatic moment of resolve; it is the result of many small, sustained choices made in pursuit of purpose. These choices may seem individually insignificant, but together they shape a life of courage. The threshold faced today requires one step forward, and tomorrow will require another. Each step is an expression of the same courage, refined by the choices made before.

You do not need to see the whole path. You need to take the next step. Courageous faith is not the confidence of someone who can see the end from the beginning. It is the trust of someone who has learned that the One who calls them can.

God requires courage from you. Not the courage of agreement, not the courage of performance, not the courage that is only available when the conditions are favorable. The kind of courage that moves into the unknown because the calling is clearer than the fear, and that sacrifices what it has in order to become what it was made for becomes necessary.

The unknown is where your purpose lives. You will not find it by staying where you are. You will not reach it by waiting for the full picture to be revealed before taking the first step. The picture is revealed in the walk. The provision arrives at the threshold, not before it. The ground holds under the foot that steps forward in faith and only under that next step.

The real sacrifice is demonstrated in the willingness of an open-handed release of what you have been holding is not the price of purpose. It is the shape of it. A life poured out in courageous obedience to a Divine calling is not a life diminished. It is a life finally, fully expressed. This is what you were made for not necessarily the comfort, safety or a carefully managed version of a life that never quite risked enough to discover its God given spiritual destiny. You were made for the leap. The door is open. It's your time to take it.

Courage is not the absence of fear. It is the decision, made in fear's presence, to step forward anyway.

PART TWO

Overcoming

We learn to overcome our limitations while in the PIT. The world peddles a massive lie about victory: it tells you that overcoming is a victory lap you take after you emerge into the light. We are conditioned to believe that we will finally fix our lives once our circumstances improve, once the money returns, or once the heavy cloud finally lifts. But true resilience is never forged on a comfortable stage.

Overcoming doesn't happen in the winner's circle; it happens right here in the mud, while the walls are still closing in. It is within the emptiness of the PIT where your titles, money, and external validations are completely stripped away where the raw limitations of your past are dragged into the light. Your low expectations, defensive habits, and deep-seated fear of being vulnerable are laid bare because you no longer have the luxury of hiding them behind a busy life.

To survive this space, you cannot rely on vague, emotional wishful thinking; you need operational precision. As someone who have worked professionally in leadership, in aviation, commercial construction, defense, information, military and nuclear industries I have been fortunate to spend a career evaluating and testing complex systems to isolate failure points before they trigger a catastrophe.

When you are in the PIT, and your internal operating system is malfunctioning, you must perform a functional test your own mind. This is the exact, tactical methodology I delivered in this book. We don't wait for the theater of operations to become safe before we execute a strategy. We map out the vulnerabilities in our internal code right now, establishing tight, non-negotiable mental boundaries to halt the system failure before it spreads.

Overcoming in the dark requires the daily, disciplined execution of micro-resilience. When your resources are gone and your emotional fuel tank is dry, you cannot fix your entire life in a single day, but you can master the next sixty seconds. You learn to execute a deliberate pivoting of your attention away from the deceptive data of your feelings and onto the unshakeable commands of your assignment.

This means choosing to breathe, stand, and steward whatever microscopic amount of energy you have left toward life. By forcing yourself to execute these small, precise maneuvers while your environment is still entirely black, you break the power of your limitations.

You prove to yourself that the darkness contained your body is a code which can be altered and rewritten towards a life of vibrancy.

Reflection Questions:

What limitation have I accepted as permanent that may actually be inviting me to develop a strength I have never been required to cultivate before?

When my titles, achievements, possessions, and external affirmations are stripped away, who am I and what qualities remain that no circumstance can take from me?

What recurring thought, habit, or emotional pattern repeatedly weakens my resolve, and what intentional boundary can I establish today to interrupt its influence?

What is the smallest life-giving action I can faithfully choose today that affirms I am moving toward healing instead of surrendering to despair?

Chapter Five

The Gift of Time

A Sacred Stewardship

The Gift

There is a kind of poverty that has nothing to do with money. It is the poverty of a life whose hours have been spent without intention. It is a life drifting from obligation to distraction, from habit to habit, without ever pausing to ask whether this is truly how you meant to spend the one life you were given.

Time is the only resource that cannot be replenished. Every other loss carries the possibility of recovery: a relationship can be repaired, a career rebuilt, a health crisis survived and healed. But an hour spent is gone with a finality that nothing else in human experience quite matches. We may understand this intellectually, but we rarely live as though we believe it.

This chapter focuses on the discipline and grace involved in treating time as a sacred responsibility. Rather than encouraging you to fill your schedule with more tasks, it challenges you to reflect on a deeper question: what is the true purpose of your time? When you answer this honestly and let it influence your decisions, transformation follows not only in how you spend your hours, but in who you become within them.

Misplaced Priorities

Chuck Swindoll, a pastor whose insights deeply influenced how I view time, once shared a memorable metaphor. He compared life to a coin, saying that although you have the freedom to spend it anyway you choose, you can only spend it once.

The image is simple. Its implications are worth pondering.

Every hour invested in something that does not align with your deepest values is an hour that cannot be recovered. The gap between our intentions and the way we spend that time is one of the most honest mirrors we have. We can tell ourselves we value a relationship, a calling, a spiritual practice but where our time actually goes tells a truer story. Not in what we desire, but in how we spend our days, it reveals our real priorities.

The casualties of misplaced priorities are rarely dramatic. They accumulate slowly, quietly, over time. A relationship that withers not from any single conflict but from sustained neglect. A purpose that dims not from a decisive failure but from years of postponement. An unresolved wound that festers beneath the surface of a busy life because we never made the time to tend to it to foster healing.

The gap between good intentions and honest time management is where these casualties are born. We mean to reach out. We intend to begin. We plan to address what needs addressing but not today, this week, and not while this current season is so demanding. Seasons pass, and the intentions remain in, and the life we meant to live has been spent doing something else. Considering your own inventory honestly is worth mentioning.

Where is the neglected relationship, stalled purpose, and unrealized calling? What false priorities or distractions dressed as necessity have been quietly claiming the hours that belonged elsewhere? Naming this is not comfortable. But it is the beginning of reclaiming your time.

Your life is the inventory of your time. The gap between who you intend to be and who you are being is measured, hour by hour, in how you spend your days.

Time and Physical Stewardship

Effective stewardship of the life we have been given begins, unavoidably, in our bodies. We are not disembodied spirits waiting for our real lives to begin. We are physical creatures whose capacity for spiritual depth, mental clarity, relational presence, and purposeful work depends in significant part on how we tend to this vessel that carries us.

Sleep is one of the most countercultural acts of time stewardship available to us in an age that treats exhaustion as a badge of productivity. Adequate rest is not laziness. It is the foundation on which everything else is built. A depleted body produces a depleted mind, diminished spirit, and a shortened capacity for the kind of presence that meaningful relationships and for purposeful work.

Movement is more than just a healthy routine; it shows respect for the life within our bodies and signals that our physical selves deserve attention. By making exercise a regular part of our daily lives, we build a habit of stewardship, reminding ourselves that what we have is valuable and should be cared for.

Perhaps the most countercultural practice of all is intentional stillness by carving out time, in a world saturated with digital noise for some peace and quietness. Quietness is not idle time. It is the time in which the mind declutters, perspective returns, and the quiet voice of discernment becomes audible again. These pauses are not luxuries; they are necessities.

Reclaiming Inner Peace and Purpose

The deepest work of the stewardship of our time is spiritual. It is the ongoing, intentional allocation of time to the inner life as it relates to the cultivation of self that persists beneath every role, obligation, and identity, the world assigns to us.

Spending time in places that encourage spiritual renewal such as nature, solitude, and silence is essential for staying connected to oneself. These environments allow us to step back from daily distractions and engage with deeper concerns, making such moments valuable even when their benefits aren't immediately measurable.

The soul requires space. When every hour is filled, when the schedule allows no room for stillness, the interior life slowly suffocates. Protecting time for renewal is an act of long-term wisdom, even when the short-term pressure to fill that time with more productive activity feels overwhelming.

Guarding the Mind

Spiritual stewardship also requires vigilance over what we allow to occupy our inner life. The negative self-talk that erodes self-worth, the demoralization that accumulates through chronic exposure to cynicism, despair, or contempt are not negligible. They claim territory in the mind and, over time, reshape what we believe is possible for ourselves. Protecting ourselves from these outside influences is a sensible way to care for our minds, which are part of something greater than the constant distractions around us. Dedicating time to activities that reinforce our values, which focuses on truth and goodness, isn't selfish but an act of stewardship.

One of the most profound forms of time stewardship is the intentional discovery and exercise of the gifts unique to you alone. Every person carries certain capacities for ways of seeing, creating, serving, and connecting to those around us. They are specific. And they are given not only for personal fulfillment but for contribution to something beyond ourselves.

Dedicating time to discovering what those gifts are, by cultivating them with discipline, and deploying them in service of something meaningful is one of the highest uses of the limited time we have. A life in which those gifts remain undiscovered, undeveloped, or hoarded is a life in which something irreplaceable has been lost not only to the person who carried them, but to everyone who might have been touched or graced by them.

The Source of Time and Purpose

At the foundation of all of this lies a conviction that transforms the entire frame: time is not ours. It is given. We are not owners of the hours we have been allotted but stewards of them. And stewardship, properly understood, carries both freedom and responsibility. When we move from seeing ourselves as owners of time to seeing ourselves as stewards, our entire approach changes. While an owner uses their possessions however they wish, a steward carefully manages what is entrusted to them, mindful of its true purpose. This shift prompts us to ask not just, "How do I want to spend my time?" but also, "What is this time meant for?"

Organizing our time in alignment with a broader purpose is not simply an exercise in religious practice. Rather, it reflects a trust that our hours contribute to goals greater than our individual priorities. This approach entails openness to guidance and a readiness to relinquish the habit of occupying every moment solely with personal gain, allowing space for direction beyond one's own initiatives.

Prayer and solitude are also primary practices through which this alignment is cultivated. Not as obligations to be discharged, but as avenues of genuine communication with the source of both time and purpose. The person who consistently makes space for this kind of communion does not become less productive. They become more discerning and better able to distinguish between what is merely urgent and what is actually important, between the activities that fill a life and the ones that give it meaning.

Learning to Understand Time Differently

My own understanding of time was reshaped gradually, through a combination of instruction and hard experience.

The turning point came through a simple church message that instructed us to set goals and not waste time. It sounds straightforward. But for someone who had been living largely by osmosis by moving through the days in response to what arose rather than in pursuit of what mattered was quietly revolutionary. It made perfect sense for the first time. I started viewing time not simply as a passive backdrop for living, but as a precious gift that comes with responsibility.

The metaphor of a coin made me realize something I had only understood in theory before: I was using the one coin of my time, often without consciously considering what I was gaining in exchange for it. Time was the currency used in the transaction. This newfound awareness took me back to an early memory when I was about six years old, I sensed what I can only call the presence of God for the first time.

That night, I went to bed full of questions I didn't yet know how to put into words: Who is God? Who am I? What does it all mean? At that moment, I felt truly alive not just in the usual way, but as if something far deeper had been awakened within me.

My life since then has been, in its truest sense, a continuation of that night. Every season of confusion, the PIT, and every mountain climb have been part of the long answer to those childhood questions. It has taken me thirty years to begin to understand what I was asking. Thirty years of eliminating distractions, reorienting priorities, learning to see the hours of my life as the medium through which that original encounter with the sacred continues to unfold. Time is valuable because it doesn't last forever.

Our use of time is the truest measure of how much we value the life we've been given.

This chapter invites you to pause and consider whether your use of time truly reflects your values and, if not, what changes are needed.

Drifting through life without intention is itself a decision which means allowing circumstances to steer your path. In contrast, living deliberately involves choosing each day to invest your time and energy in what truly matters to you.

You are spending your time right now. The question is simply whether you are spending it on purpose.

Time is God's most intimate gift.
What we do with it is our most honest answer.

CHAPTER SIX

The Breakthrough

Aligning Spirit and Purpose

Divine Alignment

When human effort ends, divine alignment begins.

There comes a point when perseverance meets surrender when all the pushing, reaching, and striving gives way to a quiet trust in something greater. This is the moment in a sacred space where inner effort merges with

Divine timing, and life begins to align with its intended purpose. I call this a breakthrough. Breakthroughs are not random, lucky, or simply driven by determination. It emerges when a person stands read inwardly open, outwardly prepared, and spiritually attuned to the subtle movement of divine assistance. This alignment creates a condition of the spirit in which transformation becomes possible not because circumstances have changed, but because we have. Breakthroughs aren't always dramatic as they may come quietly as an insight or a pivotal encounter. Regardless of form, they stem from a spirit of expectation and belief that good things are unfolding in our favor even amid uncertainty. This chapter focuses on recognizing and embracing such moments rather than simply celebrating them.

My Turning Point

In my thirties, I had a stable career and financial independence but still felt unfulfilled. What I sought was not status or achievement, but a life where my internal and external worlds matched.

Breakthroughs rarely happen during moments of celebration; they usually emerge when we reach mental exhaustion, revealing our limits and opening the door for spiritual insight. My moment came when I was standing alone on a beach in Southern California, watching the waves move in and out patiently in a sequence, I had not yet learned to practice. I had been striving for connection, purpose, and the life I sensed was possible but seemed out of reach through my efforts alone. At that moment I realized I needed to stop striving.

I spoke aloud to the vastness before me: *"Lord, if being single is Your will, I accept it. But if You have someone for me, I will wait for her in your time."*

That simple prayer was the most genuine thing I'd said in years. I was exhausted from trying to force, manipulate, persuade, and endure my way through life. This honesty brought a quiet peace and a sense of release from trying to control outcomes beyond my reach.

Leaving that beach, I felt transformed not due to any outward changes, but because my heart finally chose to trust instead of resisting. That's when I stopped struggling and began to look forward to it with hope. That was my turning point. Stillness doesn't mean doing nothing. It involves trusting, bravely letting go of control, and allowing space for Divine intervention. That preparation paves the way for breakthroughs. What appears to be idle waiting is actually a vital phase where future progress is built. Endurance fosters insight, and patience yields wisdom creating opportunities to grow in our purpose even when it seems out of sight.

In that season after the beach, I learned something that reordered my understanding of how growth works: personal effort and Divine cooperation are not opposites. They are partners. My responsibility was to become ready by cultivating emotional balance, focusing on my priorities, and doing the interior work that no external circumstances could do for me. I couldn't control the result, but I could choose to prepare. I discovered that this faith ran much deeper than simply resting on circumstances that benefited me. It was a continuous commitment, evident in my persistence to be present and maintain an attitude of openness, even when there were no obvious signs of hope. And then, quietly, things began to shift.

Coincidences accumulated in ways that felt intentional. Small confirmations didn't arrive dramatically, but unmistakable to someone who had learned to pay attention. Sometimes, Divine alignment hides entirely behind ordinary circumstances on a United Airlines employee shuttle bus, a brief conversation; and the casual exchange of contact information.

It was 2001, weeks after the September 11 terrorist attacks. The atmosphere at Chicago's O'Hare International Airport, where I worked as an aircraft maintenance supervisor, was heavy with collective grief and uncertainty. At the end of a long shift, I boarded the employee shuttle bus, tired but settled in a way I hadn't felt in years. She was already seated a flight attendant returning from a long trip. Her presence was calm against the backdrop of the industry's chaos. Her smile was genuine in a way that stood out. We spoke briefly. She mentioned a dream she carried: starting an image consulting business. I said, half joking, that I could probably use an image consultant. As the bus approached her stop, I asked for her contact information and she handed me her business card. The exchange took less than ten minutes.

Weeks passed before I called her. Our early conversations were sporadic, threaded between her flights, unhurried. There was an ease between us that did not need to be forced beyond a natural rhythm that I had not felt in any relationship built from striving. Eventually, we met again in person. When I arrived at her home, an older man opened the door. He looked at me for a moment, then said something I was not prepared to hear: "I know you." I said this neighborhood looks familiar to me as I thought my grandparents may have lived there when I was a toddler. I mentioned their names: Willis and Hulena.

As I stood in doorway, the older man revealed that he and my grandfather had been childhood friends since the 1940s, moving to Chicago together from Littlerock, Arkansas. They grew up on a farm together before finding work on the train. In that instant, it dawned on me that our families had shared a bond long before either of us existed. The realization was profound: decades of history had quietly intertwined our paths, setting the stage for this moment.

My relationship with my grandfather was uniquely special. He had passed away some ten years earlier, but his influence remained vivid. As my grandparents first grandchild, I was the recipient of extraordinary attention. Many cherished memories were from fishing trips, wandering the city, and simply spending time together as a toddler before they moved back to

Littlerock. These experiences shaped me deeply, and the connection felt more significant now, given how our families' histories converged.

What struck me most was the ordinariness of the circumstances; a bus ride after a routine day at work, and a simple conversation at a doorway. Yet, through these everyday moments, I recognized something Divine unfolding. It was as if the threads of our family histories and the events of that day were woven together by a purpose greater than coincidence in that both our grandfathers were more just friends but companions.

Standing in the doorway, I realized that I was part of a carefully crafted design. This wasn't mere coincidence or random chance it was lineage, a connecting thread stretching across generations to place me, precisely where I needed to be. This was the sign I had been waiting for not some dramatic miracle from above, but a man at a door, invoking names from my history into my current life, affirming that my journey had been mapped out long before I set foot on it.

In the wake of the 9/11 terrorist attacks, what began on a shuttle bus deepened into something neither of us had to engineer. Trust built naturally. Laughter came easily. Six months after that first bus ride, we eloped in St. Petersburg, Florida. It was simple, quiet, and exactly right beginning our future together. She was my breakthrough and a dream-maker. A year later, we started our family and that was a long time ago.

That union was the physical manifestation of everything the long season of waiting had been building toward. Not just the fulfillment of a longing for companionship though it was that too, but the confirmation of something deeper: that patience, when sustained by faith, yielding a result which striving alone never could. The breakthrough I had been prepared for had arrived, and it was specific, meaningful, and more precisely timed than anything I could have imagined.

The change radiated outward into every aspect of my life. The weight of the past, which had held authority over my decisions for years, began to lose its grip. I was not merely happy. I was restored. And restoration, unlike happiness, does not depend on circumstances remaining favorable. A breakthrough isn't a finish line it's actually a starting point, a springboard for what's next. With it comes a new responsibility: the chance to create something that honors the opportunity you've been given.

Moving Forward

As I entered this new season, I understood that every stage of the journey including the surrender on the beach, the patient waiting, and the old man at the door had not been preparation for arrival. It had been preparation for living. The point was never to receive and rest. It was to receive and move forward with greater clarity, intentionality, and a deeper sense of what I was actually here to do.

By now, I've come to understand that faith isn't just a feeling; it's a choice and an ongoing commitment. It means staying open to guidance, even when it doesn't make logical sense, and trusting enough to keep moving forward, even if the way ahead isn't clear. Faith is something you practice actively because it's not about waiting passively. It involves recommitting both to the alignment that led to breakthroughs and to the routines that help maintain that progress once the excitement of change settles into everyday life.

When life grows quiet again after a breakthrough as it always does, that is precisely when the deeper work begins.

Principles of Alignment

Through this journey, I have come to understand that breakthroughs are not one-time events. They are the rhythms establishing a moment of alignment preparing the ground for the next. What follows are not rules but recognitions of the principles I carry forward from everything the journey has taught me.

Anticipation opens the doorway to insight. Expectancy is the sustained belief that something is being prepared even when nothing is yet visible when the opportunity draws near in ways that resignation cannot. This is not wishful thinking. It is a posture of the spirit, maintained through practice, that keeps us available to what is already moving toward us.

Work hard, prepare, improve, stay active, and get ready. Recognize that effort alone is incomplete without surrender. Human effort creates the conditions, but Divine cooperation fills them. Look for quiet answers, not only dramatic ones. The most significant moments arrived without an announcement.

Growth is naturally boundless. As we heal and become more aligned, the lessons we've learned can benefit those around us. True influence comes from living as an example rather than telling others what to do. When someone transforms and lives in a new way, it encourages others to change too. This might be the greatest act of generosity we can offer.

A breakthrough signals action. Instead of treating it only as proof of success, use it as a springboard to grow, helping others pursue new goals. The discipline that got you here is essential for ongoing progress remember, arrival is not the same as completion.

Gratitude sustains alignment. Every moment of clarity, fortunate convergence, or healing carries the fingerprints of something beyond our own competence and ambition. Acknowledging this is not humility for its own sake, but it is the continuation of connection. The moment we recognize that our advancement has always been guided, we remain open to the next chapter of growth. Gratitude keeps the fertile ground alive.

There are no guarantees in life. But alignment ensures that even uncertainty carries purpose. When we meet the unknown with expectancy and honesty, when we balance persistence with surrender, breakthroughs cease to be rare events and become an ongoing dialogue between our spirit and the unseen fosters a conversation which does not end.

Each breakthrough is an awakening: a reminder that we have never been truly alone in the work of becoming whole. The path was always being prepared. The provision was always nearby. The connection we longed for was, in some cases, already written into our lineage before we were born.

The true breakthrough is not the event itself. It is the awareness which arrived through years of preparation, surrender, and attentiveness through a journey has always been guided. That every step, even the painful ones, even the ones that felt like detours, leads us toward harmony.

When readiness meets timing, life opens. When trust meets effort, transformation begins. And when acknowledgment meets gratitude, purpose sustains itself not as a destination finally reached, but as a way of moving through the world collaborating with the Divine.

The breakthrough is the moment I realized that I needed to wait on God.

CHAPTER SEVEN

Beyond the Shadows

The Decision to Rise from Depression

The Choice to Decide

Depression is especially cruel because it not only brings pain but also makes that pain feel familiar and almost comforting.

This is the truth that most accounts of depression leave out. We speak of the darkness as something imposed from outside, a condition that descends without invitation and holds us against our will. And it is true that depression is not chosen in any simple sense. But at some point, in the long inhabiting of it, something shifts. The pain can seem familiar because the confinement becomes comfortable in its own terrible way. The walls of the PIT, which once felt like a prison, begin to feel like the only place where the terms of your existence are known and manageable.

This chapter is about the moment when that changes. It's about the slow, costly, and profoundly personal decision to rise from depression. The ascension is not because the pain has ended, but because the desire for a different life has finally grown stronger than the fear of leaving the life you have been living. It is about what that decision requires, the cost, and what becomes possible on the other side of making it.

Depression is complex. For many people it has neurological, chemical, and environmental dimensions that require professional and medical support, and there is no wisdom in dismissing those realities. But there is also a dimension of depression that is interior, volitional, and spiritual. A dimension that no medication alone can fully address. It is that dimension this chapter explores: the role of choice, courage, and faith in the long work of rising.

Before we can leave this mental space, we need to understand honestly why we have stayed. This is not a comfortable question. It is far easier to describe depression as something done to us as a force that holds us against our will. Rather than examining the ways in which we participate in our own captivity. Honest examination is necessary, because the forces that keep us in stagnation are real, and they are powerful, and they will not be overcome by someone who has not yet acknowledged them.

The Adaptation Paradox

As human beings, we are extraordinarily adaptive creatures. We can adjust to almost any set of conditions, given enough time including conditions that make us miserable. This capacity for adaptation is, in most circumstances, a profound gift. In the context of depression, it becomes a trap. Over time, we adapt to the PIT. We learn its rhythms, textures, and the quality of pain. We develop coping mechanisms some healthier than others that allow us to function within its confines. We may encounter genuine moments of insight, experience true connections with the Divine, and find meaning even amid darkness. These fleeting yet significant experiences can unintentionally encourage us to remain where we are. If there is some light present, one might reason that taking the risk to seek complete illumination may be unnecessary.

This is called the adaptation paradox which can be characterized as the very resilience that helps us survive the PIT can also become the mechanism which causes us to stay longer than we need to. There is another dynamic at work that is even harder to name honestly: the way depression can function as protection.

When we are suffering, certain demands are suspended. Expectations are lowered. The pressure to perform, succeed, and show up fully in the world can ease when depression makes fulfillment seem impossible. There is a kind of safety in this, however painful. This depressed state becomes a shield against the risks of engagement which is simply trying and failing, hoping and being disappointed, and stepping into the light and finding that the light does not transform everything we feared it would. This is real stuff.

This is not a conscious calculation. It is the psyche's reasonable, if ultimately self-defeating, attempt to manage risk. Recognizing and naming it honestly rather than defending against the naming is one of the most important steps in the process of leaving the PIT. The shield that protected us has become the prison that confines us.

The Patterns That Perpetuate

Beneath both the adaptation and the shield lie specific, recurring patterns, ways of thinking, relating, and responding that keep the cycle of depression running long after the original precipitating circumstances have changed.

These patterns are often invisible precisely because they are so deeply habitual. They feel less like choices and more like facts of reality.

Identifying them requires a quality of honest, sustained self-observation that is difficult not because we are incapable of it, but because the patterns themselves resist examination. They are invested in their own continuity. Bringing them into the light requires both courage and support: the courage to look honestly, and the support of someone like a counselor, a trusted friend, a spiritual leader who can see what we cannot objectively see about ourselves.

The act of seeking help rather than isolating further is itself the first disruption of the pattern. It is the first act of choosing differently. And that choice, however small it feels in the moment, is the beginning of everything.

I want to be direct about something that took me a long time to admit: I chose to stay in the PIT far longer than I was required to. Not all at once, and not consciously. But looking back with the clarity that time and honest reflection provide, I can see the moments when the door was open and I turned away from it. The pain had become familiar. The anguish had become, in its own strange way, comfortable. I had built an identity around it as the man in the darkness, enduring, suffering, waiting. And that identity, for all its misery, was known. Leaving it meant becoming someone I had not yet been, and that uncertainty was more frightening than the suffering I already understood.

My depression was, in part, a self-made shield. I see that now. It protected me from the vulnerability of conscientious engagement, from the risk of hope, and the exposure of fully showing up in a life that might still disappoint me. The shield was not comfortable. But it was mine, and I knew its dimensions.

What finally shifted was not a single dramatic moment, but a slow accumulation of truth becoming too heavy to carry. The growing reality of pain was not new pain, but familiar that I finally recognized as unnecessary, as chosen rather than imposed. That pain outweighed the fear of leaving. At some point, my question shifted from "How do I endure this?" to "Why am I still here?"

That question was the beginning. Not the arrival, but the beginning.

My progress toward freedom rested on two things held in tension: my own active participation in the work of transformation, and my willingness to trust that God would open the next door when I was ready to walk through it. For years, I had been asking God to change my circumstances. What I needed to ask was different: not for the circumstances to shift, but for the grace to become someone who no longer needed the PIT to feel safe.

The Trials of Transition

Leaving the PIT is not a clean break. This is one of the most important things to understand about the process, and commonly misunderstood.

We imagine that the decision to rise will be followed by a clear, unobstructed ascent. That the courage to choose differently will be rewarded with immediate confirmation. That the darkness will recede once we have committed to the light. This is not how it works. The transition out of depression is a liminal passage in a threshold space between the old way and the new, marked by the disorienting experience of being neither fully in nor fully out.

In this liminal space, there will be days that feel like progress with moments of lightness, clarity, and the sense of everything moving in the right direction. There will also be days that feel like falling backward, when the darkness reasserts itself with a familiarity that mocks the progress you thought you made. This is your mind talking but you must listen to your spirit.

Both are part of the passage. The setbacks are not evidence that the progress was illusory. They are evidence that change is real and that real change is not linear. The person who understands this from the beginning will navigate the regressions with self-compassion rather than self-condemnation, treating each stumble as information rather than verdict.

Self-compassion in this phase is not self-indulgence. Recognizing the kind of sustained effort required for transformation cannot be maintained under conditions of constant self-punishment. The inner critic that has been whispering inadequacy throughout the duration of depression does not automatically go quiet when you decide to rise. Learning how to respond with patience rather than agreement is to hear its voice without accepting its authority is among the most important skills required for the transition.

The transition is also the moment when the lessons of the PIT begin to find their outward application. The patience learned while waiting, discernment developed through the crucible, and the humility are forged in spiritual growth. Faith deepens from sustaining through something that could have broken you. These are not abstract qualities. These abilities are yours, as a result of what you've experienced. The period of transition is when you start applying them to real situations in your life.

The Courage to Change

When I finally saw clearly what was keeping me in the PIT, I also saw something that had been present the entire time: the wound beneath the wound.

My depression was not only about the circumstances that had precipitated the broken relationship or the years of spiritual displacement. Beneath those circumstances lay something older and more fundamental: a low self-esteem that had been quietly shaping everything, narrowing what I believed was possible for me, nurturing the wounds of childhood rather than healing them. I had been tending my pain as though it were something precious, feeding it the attention that might have gone toward growth.

This recognition was not comfortable. It was, however, clarifying. You cannot address a wound you have not correctly identified. And once I could see the actual shape of what I was carrying, the path forward became, for the first time, something I could imagine walking.

The patterns that had sustained my stagnation began, slowly and painfully, to lose their grip. Not because I had finally acquired enough willpower to break them, but because I had finally become willing to stop serving them.

That willingness not the willpower, but the willingness was the turning point. I was building, for the first time, the fortitude to believe in my own capacity for change. Not the brittle confidence of someone who has never been broken, but the durable faith of someone who has been broken and is choosing, with clear eyes and a sober assessment of the cost, to rise anyway.

The Power of Choice

The core message of this entire book is straightforward: you have a choice.

Not a choice about whether to feel the pain. Not a choice about whether the darkness has been real. Not a choice that erases the years spent in the PIT or minimizes what they cost. But a choice, available in every moment, about what to do with what you have been given including the suffering, the wounds, including the hard-won and irreplaceable wisdom that neither came without nor would have come any other way.

The time for lingering ends not with a dramatic announcement but with a quiet internal shift: the recognition that the season of confinement has served its purpose, that the lessons it carried have been received, and that remaining any longer is no longer refinement but avoidance. When that recognition arrives and you will know it when it does, because it feels different from the many false starts that came before it. The invitation is simply to accept it. One of the most practical and underestimated tools in the work of rising is the quality of the conversation we carry on with ourselves.

For years, the inner dialogue of depression had been a monologue of diminishment. The voice that narrated my experience with the running commentary on my worth, capability, and prospects had been shaped by years of accumulated pain. Changing that voice is not a matter of positive thinking imposed over negative reality. It is a matter of learning to speak to yourself with the same care and honesty you would offer to someone you genuinely love.

This means encouraging yourself not with false reassurances, but with honest reminders of what you have already survived, what you have already learned and proven about your own resilience. It means challenging the assumptions that depression has installed as facts. These are not facts. They are the distortions of a mind under sustained stress, and they deserve to be questioned with the same rigor we would apply to any other claim about reality.

Dreaming Again

There is a particular moment in the process of rising that I want to name, because it is both more specific and more significant than it might initially appear: the return of the capacity to dream.

I don't mean sleep dreams, though those too often improve as the interior landscape begins to settle. I mean the forward-looking imagination and the ability to picture a future that is different from the present. Dreaming to want things again and to allow hope to take up residence in your mind.

Depression, in its deepest expressions, takes this capacity away. When you are fully in the PIT, the future is not a place of possibility. Dreams of allowing yourself to imagine a life that has not yet existed is one of the clearest signs that the ascent is real.

I noticed this shift before I could fully articulate what it meant. I started dreaming about the life I wanted to build, the person I was becoming, the possibilities that had been invisible from inside the darkness. A new chapter was not just theoretically available. It was actually beginning, and I could feel its approach. The burdens of the past were losing their authority over my present decisions. The past did not disappear but, I was no longer paralyzed from a place of brokenness.

The decision to rise from depression is not a single, definitive act, but rather an ongoing process. Each time you choose to move forward, even in small ways, the act of choosing itself becomes just a little easier, a little more instinctive. These repeated decisions gradually carve out new neural pathways, slowly establishing a different way of being. The transformation occurs not through dramatic gestures, but through the steady, unremarkable choices made each day. In these ordinary moments, the person you are becoming is quietly, steadily constructed, choice by choice, and day by day.

The process of recovery does not happen in an instant. The remnants of darkness linger, but they gradually relinquish their hold. Light returns in increments, much like the slow rising of the sun at the start of a new day. This return is so subtle that the precise moment it begins is impossible to pinpoint. Yet, as time passes, there comes a realization that the world is no longer shrouded in darkness.

You have always had a choice. The question is whether you were ready to make it.

Chapter Eight

The Overcomer's Path

Transforming Weakness into Strength

The Overcomer

Weakness is not the opposite of strength it is more often its origin. Traits like impatience, a need for control, anger when threatened, or fear leading to regrettable actions do not mean there is something inherently wrong with us. They are evidence that something unaddressed is still living inside us, waiting to be transformed rather than merely suppressed.

Transforming weakness into strength is among the most demanding work a human being can undertake. It requires a quality of honest self-examination that most of us spend a considerable amount of energy avoiding. It means being open to seeing ourselves and letting those closest to us see us honestly, without hiding behind denial or making excuses. A strong spiritual foundation is needed to support us as old systems are dismantled and replaced by something more aligned.

This chapter explores the transformation journey and the challenges faced, the inner and outer changes it brings, and the purpose that guides and shapes the process.

The Crucible of Transformation

Every meaningful change begins with a recognition of a moment when the gap between where we are and where we need to be become impossible to ignore. This recognition might arrive as a persistent sense of unease, a pattern we finally see clearly enough to name, or a crisis that strips away the comfortable stories we have been telling ourselves about who we are.

Merely acknowledging the situation does not constitute transformation; rather, it serves as an invitation to initiate change.

Change requires identifying the underlying problem, not just its symptoms. Without this focus, our efforts remain ineffective. Clearly naming the root issue such as a specific fear, mindset, or recurring patterns of hurt allows us to address what truly needs changing.

Transformation requires belief in our own capacity to change, and in the support available to us. Neither is automatic. The belief in our ability to truly grow involves more than just surface-level changes it requires deep, structural transformation that often needs to be nurtured, even when our past suggests we tend to repeat ourselves. This is where faith, both in God and ourselves, becomes not a comfort but a necessity.

Sometimes setbacks happen and they are not interruptions to the process but part of it. The process of overcoming challenges is seldom linear because it is different for each person. Those who recognize this early on are better equipped to manage setbacks with greater resilience compared to those who anticipate or expect uninterrupted progress. Each setback carries information. Each failure, examined honestly rather than defended against, reveals something about where the work still needs to go.

Being adaptable throughout it all gives us the ability to recognize when a strategy has stopped working and to adjust without abandoning the goal is what separates those who eventually break through from those who stay stuck. Rigidity and transformation cannot coexist. The overcomer learns, often through painful experience, to hold the destination firmly and the method loosely.

Overcoming Made Visible

Transformation begins internally, yet its effects are visible beyond the mind. The body responds to change with a precision that the mind may be reluctant to accept.

When we break through a pattern that has held us like releasing grief we have been carrying, confronting a fear we have been cultivating, or dismantling a habit that has been costing us too much creates shift which unleashes an unmistakable physical sensation. Lightness fills the chest and shoulders as chronic tension fades. Sleep becomes easier, and breathing flows more freely.

These reactions aren't just accidental they're signs. The body reveals the truth about what's happening inside, even when the mind is still trying to rationalize things. When real change takes place, the body senses it before the mind fully understands.

The reverse is also true. As we adopt the disciplines that support inner growth like intentional movement, adequate rest, the practices that quiet the nervous system and create space for reflection the body becomes a collaborator in the process rather than simply a vehicle carrying the mind from place to place.

Intentional movement, such as daily physical activity, helps both the body and mind remain connected and responsive. Adequate rest allows the body to recharge and process the changes occurring internally. Practices that calm the nervous system, like breathing exercises or periods of quiet reflection, create the necessary space for deeper transformation to unfold. In this way, the body does not merely accompany the mind; it actively participates in the journey of overcoming, offering confirmation and support for the inner work being done.

When these disciplines are embraced, the body signals its alignment with the transformation taking place. Physical sensations, such as relaxation and ease, become evidence of progress. The body, once seen only as a means of transport, becomes a vital partner, reinforcing and amplifying the breakthroughs achieved within.

Tending to the physical with the same intentionality we bring to the spiritual is not a distraction from the deeper work. It is part of it.

And perhaps most significantly: as inner patterns shift, fear loses its grip on the body. The racing heart, the constricted breath, the physical paralysis that once accompanied certain situations gradually diminish. Not because the challenges disappear, but because we are no longer meeting them with the same unexamined terror. Physical freedom from fear's grip is one of the most tangible confirmations that the overcomer's path is working.

Tending the Inner Landscape

The mind is where the seeds of transformation are planted, tended, and either allowed to grow or quietly starved of the attention they need. It is the arena in which our deepest patterns live from the beliefs formed in childhood, narratives constructed from pain, and limitations we have accepted as facts creating pathways in our lives.

Meaningful, enduring transformation involves more than simply modifying actions. It also demands an exploration of the underlying narratives: the convictions motivating those behaviors, the anxieties safeguarding them, and the original hurts that made such responses essential. This is slow, uncomfortable work. It cannot be rushed, and it cannot be completed by willpower alone. It requires a sustained willingness to sit with what is uncomfortable long enough to actually understand it.

A forward-thinking mindset is vital not to ignore the past, but to avoid being constrained by it. Overcomers learn from history and focus on future possibilities, acknowledging the past but refusing to let it define their future.

The outcome of this introspective process may be imperfect, continual, and never entirely finished; however, it ultimately leads to a state of acceptance and peace with oneself. This is not the peace that comes from resolving every conflict or healing every wound, but rather the peace found in authentic self-acceptance: an acknowledgment of one's own worthiness for compassion, an understanding that imperfections are not disqualifying, and a recognition that personal growth justifies the challenges it entails. Inner peace isn't something earned after completing a journey; it grows each day as you embrace the journey itself.

Divine Guidance in the Overcoming

Underneath the physical and mental aspects of transformation exists the spiritual dimension, which represents the most profound level. It is at this layer that foundational changes take place and where essential resources for the entire process are ultimately derived.

Engaging the spirit means extracting the lessons embedded in our experiences rather than simply enduring them. Every season of struggle carries wisdom. Every failure contained a test. The practice of reflection is a honest and unhurried process of turning raw experiences into usable understanding. This isn't rumination; it's an excavation, and when approached thoughtfully, it can reveal something valuable.

Spiritual discernment is the capacity to perceive what is true beneath what is merely loud or urgent. It is cultivated through prayer, stillness, and the willingness to wait. It is the ability to distinguish between the guidance that arises from our own anxiety and the quieter direction that comes from somewhere deeper. This discernment does not develop quickly. It is the product of a sustained spiritual practice, of accumulated experiences revealing what was understood over time.

One of the most liberating discoveries of a spiritual life is the freedom that comes from releasing the need to control outcomes. This isn't indifference;

it means preparing and acting responsibly, while understanding that outcomes depend on a greater wisdom than ours. Entrusting our battles to the Divine does not remove us from the arena. It changes how we fight: with less desperation, more clarity, and a steadiness that does not depend on whether things are unfolding according to our plan.

Throughout the journey, maintaining a patient and trusting mindset helps us progress even when hope seems distant. This expectancy is not wishful thinking. It is a practiced faith, refined through the accumulated experience of having waited and seen the provision arrive.

How Overcoming Actually Works

The overcomer's path is not a concept. It is a sequence of concrete choices, made in the ordinary conditions of ordinary life, that accumulate over time into a genuinely different person.

It begins in the quietness with inner determination and a foundational commitment to see the process through regardless of how long it takes. This is the bedrock. Without it, every subsequent effort is viewed with discouragement.

The hardest part is starting. It's not about just planning or waiting for perfect conditions, but about actually taking action even when you are unsure. Familiar routines are hard to break, but even small actions can build momentum. Each step makes the next one easier.

Planning and learning are tools that give determination of its direction. By recognizing the challenge, assessing available resources, and crafting a deliberate plan, you avoid wasting energy on unfocused tasks which achieve little. However, planning should always support action and not replace it.

When failure comes, an overcomer's response is the difference between growth and stagnation. Instead of ignoring failure or exaggerating its consequences, we should honestly explore what it can teach us. Failure is data. The question is not whether to be discouraged by it, but whether to let the discouragement be the end of the sentence or merely a comma in a longer one.

Throughout the process, willpower isn't about gritting your teeth or denying yourself; it's about developing the ability to consistently follow through with your commitments, even when you feel strongly tempted to revert to old habits. This is a muscle, and like all muscles, it strengthens through use. Every time you choose the harder right thing over the easier familiar thing, the next choice becomes marginally less difficult. This is how character is formed not in a dramatic sense of resolution, but in the accumulated weight of small, consistent choices made in the direction of who you are becoming.

The Divine Blueprint

Within a framework of faith, transformation is understood not as self-improvement but as alignment the gradual conforming of our actual lives to a design that existed before we were aware of it. This reframes everything. The question is not only "what do I need to change?" but "why is this change necessary?"

Seeking the why behind a transformative call is the beginning of the motivation to move in towards alignment. Not the surface-level why of wanting to feel better or perform better, but the deeper why of purpose and calling. This inquiry requires prayer, reflection, and a willingness to sit with questions that do not resolve quickly. The why that sustains a long transformation is rarely the one that first presents itself. It deepens with time, as we begin to understand not just what we are being called away from, but what we are being called toward.

Divine timing is one of the most difficult realities of a spiritual life to accept and one of the most liberating, once we do. Our impatience with our own growth is understandable. But the recognition that certain transformations unfold according to a timetable we did not set, and cannot accelerate through sheer force of will, brings a particular kind of peace. It relocates our responsibility from control to readiness. We cannot determine when the season will turn. We can determine whether we will be prepared when it does.

Divine guidance manifests in practical ways that begin with attentiveness. This means actively listening to the counsel of those with greater wisdom, observing the recurring patterns within our own lives, and paying attention to the subtle promptings that arise in moments of prayer and stillness. Such attentiveness forms the foundation of spiritual discernment and is the gateway to recognizing the guidance that is available to us.

Responding to Divine guidance is not a one-time event but an act of ongoing obedience. This obedience is not about submitting to an external authority that demands compliance; rather, it is about aligning with a wisdom that, when followed, consistently leads us toward greater wholeness.

The journey often requires us to step into unfamiliar territory into places where our own skills and confidence are insufficient. In these moments, we are invited to rely on something greater than ourselves, trusting that the path, though uncomfortable, is shaping us in profound ways.

This process, though challenging, is precisely the point. Divine guidance does not promise comfort or ease, but it does offer the opportunity for growth, transformation, and a deeper sense of wholeness that emerges as we continually respond to its call.

The Necessary Chaos

Some of us are born into chaos we did not choose. The patterns of our parents, the environments that shaped us, the identities we were handed to us before we could evaluate them. These become the invisible architecture of our interior lives. Unexamined, they drive us. Examined honestly, they become the material of transformation.

For me, the chaos took a specific shape. My dysfunction manifested primarily as a two-fold personality defect: impatience and the compulsive need to control. I want to be honest about that not as confession for its own sake, but because naming the actual problem is the only path to addressing it. My wife, who holds a master's degree in counseling psychology, has observed this list and can probably suggest more than two, and she would be very likely correct.

The roots of these traits ran deep. They were reinforced through adolescence and cemented during my years in the military, where control and impatience were not defects but assets until they were no longer. It took years of pain, and the particular clarity from watching how my patterns affect the people I loved most and to finally see myself as I actually was rather than how I imagined myself.

My wife's training in mental health, combined with her willingness to speak honestly with patience, was not always received gracefully, but it gave me a lens to see myself in ways I could not have developed alone. This is what trusted relationships do when we allow them to: they show us ourselves. The reflection is not always flattering. It is, however, necessary.

Once I could see clearly, the next question was what to do with what I saw. Validation alone is not transformation. Understanding your dysfunction conceptually is not the same as doing the work of changing it. Personally, this work demanded spiritual discipline, true humility, and an acceptance that I couldn't resolve the issue with the same determination and self-reliance that, in many respects, caused the problem initially.

My path toward that humility wound led me through unexpected territory. Something inside me confirmed that I needed to go deeper with God. I wanted a closer encounter with God, so I embarked on a three-day water fast as an act of spiritual purification. The first day of the fast was the hardest because I didn't know what to expect. The second day was much better because my system was adjusting to skipping six meals in a row. I would go for long walks at the Dana Point Habor in California. It's a beautiful place to connect with nature near the ocean.

There was noticeable clarity in my mind which is quite difficult to explain with words. I felt like I was more attuned to the spirit as my energy level also increased. I wanted more, so I volunteered for a twelve-month assignment in the Middle East. I needed some isolation what I would describe as my own personal pilgrimage.

My assignment took me to Kuwait, Bahrain, and Oman had already begun reshaping my understanding. I was immersed in Islamic tradition waking each morning in Bahrain to the call to prayer, watching hundreds of men worship God in the open air, observing the communal discipline of Ramadan. What I encountered there was not foreign. It was recognizable.

The devotion, the surrender, the ordering of daily life around the acknowledgment of the Divine spoke to something I had always carried but not always known how to name. It was a way of life. The culture was captivating, with people living at a different pace than in many Western societies. In Oman, camels roamed the busy streets freely, and their naturally sweet milk offered a unique experience.

Ramadan was a month-long special practice where we all were expected to abstain from food and water during daylight. You could be arrested if you were caught drinking water or eating in public. Many Bahraini families would leave their homes during this season to stay in vibrant, well-decorated tents in the desert, joining hundreds of other families. When night falls and the sun sets, they gather individually for a feast which celebrates the beauty of Islam. Gathered around bonfires, they celebrated each night in the desert darkness. I loved the peace and tranquility of the culture.

One year after returning home, in pursuit of greater spiritual insight, I became acquainted with the Bahá'í faith. The Bahá'í faith traces its spiritual origins to Zoroastrianism a Persian religion some 4000 years ago. The faith is a 19th-century global religion emphasizing the unity of all people and the essential oneness of all religions. The Bahai faith's central conviction is that the world's great spiritual traditions are different expressions of a single Divine truth. This resonated with everything my own journey had taught me.

During this moment of searching, it was important to understand how other people practiced their faith. I frequently met with some deacons from the Church of Latter-Day Saints. Members believe in God, Jesus Christ, and the Holy Ghost. They view Jesus Christ as the Savior of the world and follow His teachings as outlined in the Bible and the Book of Mormon, which they consider another testament of Jesus Christ. My time spent with the community was uniquely spiritual. I loved visiting the church and enjoyed the fact they embraced me sometimes being the only black person in a sea of white faces. I felt the power of the spirit and their loving kindness.

What these encounters gave me, ultimately, was not a new religion. They gave me a cleaner access to the God I had always known. The same God who touched me at six years old, asking questions I couldn't yet articulate. The same God who met me in the PIT, on the beach, at the door of a stranger who knew my grandparents' names. My path had brought me full circle back to the beginning, coupled with thirty years of hard-won wisdom about who I was and what my mission is to humanity.

It is simply God and me now. Not the God of a particular institution and religion, but the God who has been present in every tradition I have encountered, and in every season of my life.

Your personality defects are not your identity. They are unaddressed chaos waiting to be named. Identify one negative pattern of impatience, fear, the need for control and commit to engaging it honestly this week. Don't ask God to remove what you will not face. Ask God to empower you to confront the chaos you have been perpetuating and trust that the confrontation itself is the beginning of the cure.

The overcomer's path is not a path walked once and completed. It is the ongoing, daily practice of choosing growth over the comfort of the familiar, honesty over the protection of self-deception, and trust in the Divine over self-reliance.

Your weaknesses do not disqualify you; they represent the foundation of strength. Facing your patterns honestly and engaging with the challenges shapes you into an overcomer: not someone without struggle, but someone who refuses to let struggle define them.

The path is long. The work is real. And you are more capable than you know.

PART THREE

Depression

Consider reframing this thought, "You are not a depressed person; you are a whole person currently navigating a depressed landscape."

We must begin by stripping away the toxic, suffocating layer of shame that the world splashes onto mental distress. Somewhere along the line, a dangerous lie took root: the idea that if you are a person of faith, or if you are mentally strong, you should be completely immune to the heavy darkness . We are told that feeling crushed means we are spiritually broken, that our prayers lack power, or that our character is fundamentally flawed. But I am here to tell you that this weight is not a penalty, nor is it an anomaly.

Depression is not the whole of life, but it is undeniably part of the human experience. Like grief, disappointment, illness, and loss, it visits lives without discrimination. It is not proof that you are broken; it is evidence that you are participating in the difficult, beautiful, and unfinished work of being human.

If you look closely at the architecture of our existence, you will see that darkness is a structural component of the journey. By naming depression as a passing season rather than your permanent identity, you fundamentally alter your relationship with the pain. You are not a depressed person;

you are a whole person currently navigating a depressed landscape. When a brutal winter rolls in, you do not look at the snow and conclude that the sun has ceased to exist or that the earth is fundamentally frozen, you simply recognize that the environment has changed and you make the necessary adjustment for the season. Normalizing this weight clears the distorted lens of your perception. It allows you to say, "It is dark today, and it feels heavy, but this is just the current weather pattern of a particular season that will ultimately change in due time."

Reflection Questions:

Have I mistaken a painful season for my permanent identity, and how might my I see this darkness as a chapter rather than the entire story?

What shame have I carried because of my depression, and does this struggle mean I am weak, faithless, or somehow less worthy of love?

When I look back across my life, what previous seasons of suffering have eventually given way to growth, wisdom, compassion, or unexpected purpose?

Who am I beneath this season of pain, and what enduring truths about my identity remain unchanged even while my emotional landscape feels dark?

Chapter Nine

Cultivating the Mind

The Journey to Renewal

The Necessity of Change

In pursuit of a mindset renewal often stems from a profound "Why" rooted in a deep-seated realization for the necessity for change. This recognition can arise from a growing awareness of persistent dissatisfaction, a nagging sense that life is not unfolding in alignment with one's true potential, or a dawning understanding that current ways of thinking are hindering growth and well-being.

Exploring the underlying reasons for this need whether it's a desire for greater joy, improved relationships, enhanced personal effectiveness, or a deeper sense of purpose provides the motivation to embark on the often-challenging journey of mindset transformation. This justification acts as an internal compass, guiding us through the inevitable obstacles and reinforcing our commitment to creating a more fulfilling and authentic existence.

Often, the impetus for seeking mindset renewal arises from the disconnect between intention and reality. Despite sincere efforts and a desire for positive outcomes, one may find themselves consistently experiencing poor results, creating a frustrating gap between their aspirations and their lived experience. This can manifest in repeated relationship failures, stagnation in personal or professional growth, or a persistent inability to achieve desired goals.

This disparity serves as an indicator that the current mindset, despite conscious intentions, is operating as a limiting factor, subtly sabotaging efforts and perpetuating undesirable outcomes. Recognizing this disconnect is a powerful catalyst for acknowledging the need for a fundamental shift in thinking and belief systems to finally bridge the gap between intention and reality and unlock the potential for meaningful change in one's life.

Furthermore, the urgent need for mindset renewal can be illuminated by the impact of toxicity in one's environment. The presence of toxic relationships, characterized by negativity, manipulation, and emotional drain, can significantly erode one's mental and emotional well-being, fostering a breeding ground for negative thought patterns and limiting beliefs. Similarly, environments marked by pain, abuse, and dysfunction create a constant state of stress and undermine self-worth, making it exceedingly difficult to cultivate a positive and growth-oriented mindset.

Recognizing the detrimental effects of this external toxicity underscores the critical need for internal renewal as a means of self-preservation and a pathway toward creating healthier boundaries and fostering environments that support, rather than sabotage, personal growth.

The recognition of the need for mindset renewal often stems from a deep awareness of the internal struggle. This inner turmoil can manifest in a hurtful mindset, characterized by persistent negative self-talk, limiting beliefs, and destructive reasoning patterns that undermine confidence and resilience. Emotionally, this struggle can present as overwhelming and destructive emotional patterns, such as chronic anxiety, persistent sadness, or volatile anger, which cloud judgment and hinder healthy responses to life's challenges.

Moreover, this internal landscape may be further characterized by a profound lack of internal character traits like commitment, endurance, fortitude, resilience, and tenacity, making it difficult to pursue goals, overcome obstacles, and sustain positive change. Recognizing this internal battleground serves as a powerful motivator for seeking mindset renewal, aiming to cultivate the internal strength and positive thought patterns necessary to navigate life's complexities with greater ease and achieve lasting personal growth and well-being.

Confronting the Label

Sometimes life challenges us to change our mindset. For me it was when living in Chicago as a teenager. The societal narrative often placed me and many of my neighbors into a limiting box: "poor, uneducated, and Black." Most of our families were trapped in their socioeconomic status; public education was substandard, and the expectation of change was dangerously low.

Then overnight the local steel industry vanished, causing severe job losses. Many households were impacted, including many white families. The collapse of the steel industry on Chicago's South-Side, including places like Harvey, wasn't caused by one single event. It was the result of several overlapping economic and structural changes in the 1970s that made the old model of American steelmaking obsolete.

Harvey's mid-20th-century economy was deeply tied to its rail connections, which linked the town to Chicago's broader industrial network. Major lines like the Illinois Central Railroad and Baltimore and Ohio Railroad ran through or near Harvey, connecting it to national markets. These railroads made the area attractive for heavy industry, especially steel manufacturing, by enabling the efficient movement of raw materials like iron ore and coal, as well as finished products.

Railroads also played a central role in daily life. The commuter service what is now the Metra Electric Line transported workers between Harvey, Chicago, and surrounding industrial suburbs. In addition, local rail yards and switching facilities provided jobs and supported nearby warehouses and factories, making rail a major source of employment beyond the steel mills themselves.

By the late 1960s and into the 1970s, however, this system began to decline. The downturn in the steel industry reduced freight demand, while trucking and the interstate highway system made rail less dominant for shipping. At the same time, railroad mergers and financial crises such as the collapse of Penn Central which led to consolidation and the abandonment of less profitable routes and facilities. As rail activity shrank, Harvey lost another key economic foundation, accelerating the broader pattern of industrial decline in the region.

In the 1980s, I felt out of place in my neighborhood and believed I was not college material. A quiet shift comes before surrender: the sense that one season is ending, old ways no longer work, and a new way of being is needed. To prepare for change is to honor that inner knowing, reflect on what has been learned, release rigid expectations, and ready the heart for a path not yet clear.

It wasn't a single decision or one policy, and it didn't happen only under one mayor but under Richard J. Daley and his successors. Chicago pursued a mix of "urban renewal," public-housing reform, and infrastructure expansion that ended up displacing many Black residents from the South Side and West Side.

City leaders wanted to clear what they labeled "blighted" neighborhoods to make way for universities, expressways, and commercial development. Projects tied to University of Illinois at Chicago and highway construction like the Dan Ryan Expressway corridor required large-scale demolition. These areas were often predominantly Black neighborhoods, so displacement fell heavily on those communities.

Early public housing in Chicago had concentrated poverty in large high-rise projects like Robert Taylor Homes and Cabrini Greens. By the late 1960s and 1970s, these developments were seen as failing. Federal policy began pushing toward lower-density housing and, later, demolition. That meant fewer units available in the city just as displacement was increasing. Chicago was and still remains highly segregated. Efforts to move Black families into white neighborhoods met strong resistance.

City leadership often steered relocation into already Black or rapidly changing areas either on the far South Side or in nearby suburbs rather than integrating other parts of the city. At the same time, many white residents were moved further west, opening up housing in south suburbs like Harvey, Dolton, and Riverdale. Those suburbs became some of the few places where Black families could move in significant numbers, whether by choice or because other options were limited.

I grew up during these times. The narrative surrounding my neighborhood was clear and relentless: poor, uneducated, and Black. Most families around us were trapped in their socioeconomic circumstances. Public education was underfunded and overextended. The expectation of genuine, structural, and personal change was extremely low. Not because the people around me lacked worth or intelligence or drive, but because the systems that shaped daily life were designed, whether consciously or not, to confirm the label rather than challenge it.

Labels are powerful not because they are true, but because they are repeated until they feel like truth. And when the repetition is thorough enough, the label migrates from something imposed from outside to something believed from within. That is when it becomes most dangerous when the prison is no longer only external but has been quietly constructed inside the mind.

I was fortunate, in ways I did not fully understand at the time, to have a counterweight.

My uncle Larry defied every dimension of the narrative. He pursued higher education. He served in the Air Force as a plumber and returned to Chicago to launch Pyramid Plumbing while earning his MBA. He was groomed by his Jewish mentors in business and contract negotiation. He was successful in ways that were visible and specific and impossible to dismiss. He drove a 1970 white Corvette Stingray. Then a Mercedes and a bunch of other cars and a Harley-Davidson motorcycle. Once a month he would stop by our house with a box of Dunkin' Donuts. While everyone was chomping on donuts, he would take me for rides around the neighborhood.

He was a young black man in his twenties living noticeably differently from all the drug dealers and gang bangers who infested my neighborhood. He was not alone. My father, grandfather, and uncles were also hard-working business owners of construction companies as cement masons, electricians, plumbers, and painters of Phoenix, Illinois. They built their own homes and constructed their lives from the ground up during the 1970s and '80s. I came from a legacy of people who made, fixed, built things. They were my informal network of mentors who demonstrated, through the simple fact of their lives, that the label was a lie.

But knowing that the label is a lie and having internalized it are two different problems. And for much of my adolescence, despite everything I could see in my family, I remained trapped inside the lie.

As a teenager, my allergies kept me confined indoors through the Chicago summers, isolated in a way that was both painful and, as it turned out, formative. Stuck in my room, I listened obsessively to WLS radio. I fell in love with rock and roll. I taught myself how to play the lead guitar by ear with the patience of someone who had nothing else to do and nowhere else to be. I did not know then that I was cultivating something a capacity for solitary discipline, for learning through repetition, for finding meaning in a confined space. I only knew I was bored and lonely and searching for something I could not yet name.

In the 1980s, I attended Thornwood High School in South Holland. Ms. Howard, my high school math teacher, asked the class a question that most teachers ask without expecting an honest answer: what do you want to do with your life when you grow up? I raised my hand and answered without hesitation: I want to be a pilot.

She did not dismiss the answer. She did something better. She took us to the school library and introduced us to the Federal Occupational Handbook. This book was reference material published by the U.S. Bureau of Labor Statistics. The handbook is like an official government "career encyclopedia." It was meant to help students, job seekers, counselors, veterans, and workers compare occupations and understand the labor market. The book explained whether the government expected the occupation to grow, stay stable, or decline over the next several years.

My research suggested that my colorblindness would disqualify me from becoming a pilot. I could have interpreted as another door closed, but I saw it differently, especially since I had never flown on an airplane. If I could not fly the plane, then maybe I could work on them as a jet engine mechanic. Ms. Howard changed my life by taking a teenager's dream seriously enough to research it.

Using uncle's home address, my parents sent me to Thornwood High School, a predominantly white school beyond our district, instead of Thornton High School, a predominantly Black school less than a mile from our house. At Thornwood, I was finally stretched by my studies, and for the first time, my mind began to feel like a way forward. I knew my way of thinking had to change, and slowly, imperfectly, it did.

The pursuit of mindset renewal begins with a recognition that most of us resist for longer than we should: the thinking that got us here is not the thinking that will take us forward. This realization hits hard because our thoughts don't feel like habits, they feel like the truth. The beliefs we've held since childhood about our worth, and our potential have hardened into facts. We've lived inside them for so long, and heard them echoed by so many voices, that questioning them feels less like an epiphany and more like an attack on our very foundation."

The gap between our intentions and our results is one of the most reliable indicators that a foundational shift is needed. When we consistently want one thing and consistently produce another when the relationships follow the same painful arc regardless of the person, when the professional efforts plateau at the same ceiling regardless of the application, when the spiritual aspirations remain aspirations rather than experience something in the underlying our thought process requires examination.

The Role of Our Environment

External environments matter more than most self-improvement frameworks acknowledge. Toxic relationships are those characterized by chronic negativity, manipulation, or the systematic undermining of worth do not just cause unhappiness. They actively shape the mental patterns through which we interpret all of our experiences. A person immersed long enough in an environment that confirms the worst about them will eventually begin to confirm it themselves.

This is not weakness. It is the mind doing exactly what minds do: learning from the patterns of experience and updating beliefs accordingly. The problem is that what the mind learns from a toxic environment is false, and the resulting beliefs, however sincerely held sabotage every subsequent effort at growth.

Recognizing the detrimental effects of external toxicity is not the same as blaming the environment for everything. It is the accurate assessment of influence that makes it possible to address the internal renewal with appropriate strategy rather than naive willpower alone. Beneath the external influences lies the internal landscape: the persistent negative self-talk, the limiting beliefs installed so early that they preceded conscious memory, the destructive emotional patterns that cloud judgment and undermine healthy response. This is the terrain that renewal most fundamentally addresses.

The recognition that this internal battleground exists and that it is operating constantly, shaping perception and driving behavior beneath the level of conscious awareness is both sobering and liberating. Sobering because the work of addressing it is genuinely demanding. Liberating because it locates the source of lasting change exactly where it resides not in external circumstances, but in the mind that interprets and how it responds to them.

The Process of Detoxification and Purification

Meaningful mindset renewal requires more than intention. It requires a deliberate, systematic clearing of the accumulated patterns, influences, and ingrained beliefs that have been shaping our experiences from below the surface. This is the work of detoxification and purification. It is not a singular event, but an ongoing practice of honest identification and intentional release.

The first step is the hardest: naming, with specific honesty, what is actually present. Not the general acknowledgment that "I have some negative thinking" or "my past has affected me," but the precise identification of the specific thought patterns, the relationships, concrete habits and environments that are actively working against growth and liberation.

This requires the kind of honest self-observation discussed in the previous chapter about the willingness to see clearly without immediately defending against what is seen. It is helped enormously by the perspective of someone who knows us well enough to see what we have normalized: a trusted counselor, a spiritually mature friend, a spouse or partner with the courage to speak honestly and the relationship to make that honesty receivable.

On the mental level, detoxification means actively addressing the negative self-talk and limiting beliefs that operate as the mind's default commentary. This is not positive thinking in the superficial sense, but the recitation of affirmations over unchanged underlying beliefs. It is the more demanding work of examining each limiting belief, tracing its origins, testing its validity against evidence, and consciously choosing a more accurate and empowering interpretation.

The subconscious mind is the deeper challenge here. The beliefs that most powerfully shape behavior are often the ones least available to conscious examination. These beliefs were formed before we had language adequate to question them; the ones absorbed from the emotional atmosphere of childhood rather than explicitly taught. Accessing and reprogramming these thoughts requires sustained practice: meditation, intentional prayer, journaling that goes below the surface, and often the guided work of a professional who understands how these patterns form and how they can be changed.

Detoxification is holistic. It is difficult to distinguish a pattern from the truth when you are standing in the center of it. Those childhood lessons on what we deserve and how the world works have become the bedrock of our identity. We've lived within those borders for so long that questioning them feels less like an intellectual exercise and more like a threat to our very survival. It is part of the work.

Spiritually, purification involves attending to what we allow to occupy the interior life: the music, the media, the conversations, the spiritual inputs that either nourish or deplete. It involves cultivating humility through the willingness to acknowledge our errors of wrongdoing, seeking forgiveness, releasing self-protective pride that keeps us from the openness and vulnerability change requires.

It involves the honest confrontation of the inner struggles of unresolved grievances, persistent fears, and patterns of behavior that we know are self-defeating and have not yet found the courage to fully address.

External relationships require the same honest assessment as internal patterns. Some relationships nourish growth; others, however longstanding or emotionally significant, actively impede it. No one is perfect but the willingness to set healthy boundaries and, when necessary, to create distance from relationships that consistently pull toward the old patterns is not selfishness. It is responsible stewardship of the inner life that genuine renewal requires.

This does not mean abandoning everyone who is imperfect, or withdrawing from relationships whenever they become difficult. It means making conscious, honest choices about whose voices are shaping your self-understanding, and whether those voices are oriented toward your growth or against it.

Embracing a Renewed Mindset

The garden metaphor beneath this chapter is both tender and true: a garden does not become fruitful because it was cleared once. It becomes fruitful through the quiet rhythm of return to the daily tending, watchful care with patient hands that keep old weeds from rising again, and loosing the soil for new roots, and making room for something living and worthy of harvest.

Mindset renewal is exactly this. It is not a one-time event. It is a practice, sustained across time, that gradually reshapes the interior landscape until the new patterns become as automatic as the old ones once were.

Renewal requires clarity of intention: knowing specifically what kind of thinking, what quality of inner life, what patterns of emotional response you are cultivating toward. Vague aspirations produce vague results. The more precisely you can articulate the specific changes being sought in how you speak to yourself, in how you respond to setbacks, in what you choose to believe about your own capacity the more effectively your daily practice can be oriented towards them.

Consistent practice is the mechanism through which intention becomes reality. New neural pathways are built through repetition, not resolution. The decision to think differently is the beginning; the daily practice of actually thinking differently while catching old patterns and choosing new ones is what eventually makes the new pattern the default.

While I was in the PIT, I found a word that gave me strength: 'fantastic.' Whenever someone asked how I was doing, I answered, 'Fantastic!' Saying it made me feel powerful."

Moving forward requires releasing the emotional grip of the past without pretending the past did not happen. This distinction matters. The goal is not amnesia but the erasure of difficult experiences as though they carry no meaning. The goal is freedom and the intentional release of emotional attachments and ingrained reactions that keep past experiences governing present choices.

We are not defined by what happened to us. We are shaped by it which is different. Shaped means influenced, informed, even permanently marked. But not imprisoned. The person who has processed their past carries its wisdom without being ruled by its wounds. The experiences that once constrained become the context for a deeper understanding of both suffering and resilience.

The Ongoing Journey

Sustaining a renewed mindset requires the cultivation of acceptance and grace toward the world, other people, and most importantly toward ourselves. The world is imperfect. People are imperfect. We are imperfect. The expectation of otherwise is not idealism; it is the setup for a resentment that will quietly poison every relationship and undermine every effort at sustained peace.

Real self-compassion has nothing to do with performance. It means holding your failures without becoming them, seeing your limits without enshrining them, and bringing to the long work of growth the one thing it cannot survive without: patience with yourself. Not as you wish you were, but as you actually are, right now, in the middle of it.

God's role in this process is not passive. The Divine provides the opportunity, time, and space for growth and more than that, which is the transformation of even our deepest pain into something useful. No experience is wasted in the spiritual economy. The wound that seemed purely destructive becomes the source of a particular compassion. The season of confinement becomes the origin of hard-won wisdom. The label that was meant to limit becomes the very thing we were formed to transcend while helping others transcend themselves.

The mind, like a garden, reveals the care it has been given. A neglected garden does not remain neutral; it returns to weeds, to the untamed path of least resistance. Weeds require no invitation, no intention, no cultivation. They were always there beneath the surface, waiting for the tending to stop.

Renewal is not the natural state toward which things drift. It is the achieved state, maintained through consistent, intentional practice. The good news is that the practice, once begun, compounds. Each small act of cultivation makes the next one slightly more natural. Each weed pulled makes the garden slightly easier to tend. Each choice toward the renewed mind reinforces the neural pathways that make the next choice more accessible.

The mind God gave you is not the limitation you are stuck with. It is the garden you are invited to tend. Start where you are. Use what you have. And trust that cultivation, faithfully practiced, will produce something worth the effort. Something that could not have grown anywhere else, from any other soil, in any other life but yours.

The mind you were given is not limited

Chapter Ten

Navigating the Currents of Change

Change is Inevitable

Change is Coming

Change is not a question of if, but when and, more importantly, how.

We prefer to believe we are in charge when change happens in our lives. That we will initiate them when we are ready, on terms we have negotiated with ourselves, at a pace we have chosen in advance. And sometimes, this is true. Sometimes change arrives as an act of will be based on a decision made from a place of genuine readiness, an intentional step toward a different life.

More often, if we are honest, change arrives uninvited. It comes as loss, failure, rejection, and the sudden dissolution of something we had counted on continuing. It comes in forms we would not have chosen and at moments we did not choose. When change comes imposed rather than invited, our first response is almost always the same: resistance.

This chapter is about that resistance, and what lies on the other side of releasing it. It is about the difference between wishing things were different and desiring to change. It is about the forced pilgrimage that involuntary change demands and why that pilgrimage, undertaken honestly, leads somewhere that voluntary change alone could never have taken us. Before we can navigate change well, we need to understand what is driving it both in the broad sense of human life and in our own specific circumstances.

Growth is not optional. It is woven into the biological, relational, and spiritual structure of our existence. An organism that stops adapting stops thriving. A relationship that stops evolving stagnates. The spirit that resists all disruption eventually becomes rigid in ways that are indistinguishable from dying. This means that change is not an interruption to life but a feature of it. Someone who grasps this concept practically, instead of just agreeing with it in theory, responds to unwanted changes from a wholly different perspective. Not with enthusiasm, necessarily. Not without grief. But with the recognition that what is being asked of them belongs to the same process that has always been responsible for their growth.

Not all changes are equal in how it arrives. Some change we initiate from inner readiness, a decision made in a season of clarity, and a courageous step toward something we have long known was necessary. This kind of change carries its own challenges, but it comes with the psychological advantage of having been chosen. We own it from the beginning.

Forced change is different. It arrives through rejection, failure, loss, betrayal, and through the collapse of something we had built our stability around. It does not ask permission. It does not measure our readiness. It carries a particular kind of pain because it was not chosen: the pain of confronting the limits of our control over our own lives.

And yet forced change is often the more transformative of the two. The change we choose tends to remain within the parameters of who we already are. The change forced upon us demands that we become someone we have not yet been. There is a reason the most significant growth in most people's lives traces back not to comfortable decisions but to devastating disruptions.

Fear is the primary force that determines how we respond to change, particularly the change we did not initiate. It manifests resistance and avoidance while making compulsive attempts to restore what has been disrupted. In this function, fear is protective trying to keep us safe from the unknown. But fear also has a secondary function which is less often acknowledged. When the pain of remaining in a stagnant situation finally exceeds the fear of moving into the unknown and the cost of staying becomes more than the cost of going, fear can become the very force that breaks the inertia. The same emotion that once kept us frozen can propel us forward.

Recognizing this dual nature of fear as both the thing we must move through and the thing that can move us is one of the most useful reorientations available on the journey through the PIT. Don't view involuntary change as punishment. The rejection, the failure, the loss these are not evidence that something has gone wrong. They are Divine instigators, moving you from a stagnation you would not have left on your own. The question is not why this happened. The question is what you will do with where it has brought you.

Navigating Change

Understanding why change is necessary does not automatically equip us to move through it well. The how to navigate change is its own discipline is a set of capacities and orientations that must be cultivated intentionally, because they do not arise naturally in the presence of disruption.

The process of change is an emotional journey. There is no version of forced transition that bypasses grief, disorientation, anger, confusion, and the alternating currents of hope and despair. Attempts to skip or suppress these emotional realities rarely succeed. They simply postpone what will inevitably need to be addressed, usually waiting until the issue has grown strong enough to cause real disruption.

Acceptance here is not resignation. It is the honest acknowledgment of what is real, including the full emotional weight of the disruption as the necessary foundation for movement toward the right direction. You cannot adapt to a reality you have not acknowledged. You cannot integrate an experience you have spent your energy denying. The willingness to feel what the change has actually costs is not weakness.

It is the prerequisite for everything that follows.

Navigating change well requires more than endurance. It requires creativity and the willingness to think differently about what is possible, to question the assumptions that the previous arrangement had made invisible, and to find approaches that the old situation would never have demanded.

This is one of the genuine gifts concealed within forced change: it disrupts the defaults. The job loss forces a reconsideration of what work is actually for. The relationship's end forces an encounter with a self that had been partially defined by the relationship. The health crisis forces a reckoning with what actually matters. These disruptions are painful because they provide clarity in ways that comfort alone cannot.

Adaptation that is creative does not simply restore what was lost in a different form. It builds something that could only have been built from the rubble of something old that would not have existed without the disruption that made it necessary.

Spiritual Orientation

When approaching change with faith, people often wonder not just how to manage it practically but also what its deeper purpose might be. They ask themselves what is required of them and how the experience is shaping their character or beliefs.

This orientation does not make change painless. It makes it more meaningful, which is different in the long run, and more sustainable. The conviction that even forced change operates within a larger Divine purpose does not eliminate grief, but it can prevent despair. It holds open the possibility that what feels like destruction might actually be a process of creation, seen from a perspective we have yet embraced.

Prayer in these seasons becomes less about asking for the change to be reversed and more about asking for the wisdom to navigate it faithfully. The surrender that prayer requires the release of the demand that things unfold according to our preference is itself one of the most important acts of adaptation available to us. Recognizing the right time to act during periods of change is more a matter of intuition than exact science. It's when your inner sense of readiness matches the needs around you. When staying where you are becomes even more uncomfortable than taking the step to move ahead. This moment cannot be forced. However, it can be anticipated.

The person who has been doing the interior work by processing grief and examining patterns while cultivating the willingness is readied sooner than the one who has been resisting the process. Preparation does not guarantee the right time it ensures that when the time comes, you are available to meet it.

The Spirit of Appreciation

After painful, forced change, something unexpected can emerge: an appreciation for what the disruption made possible. Not gratitude for the pain itself, not a romanticizing of suffering, but the honest recognition that what you now carry the resilience, self-knowledge, and wisdom from having genuinely struggled would not exist without the change that felt, at the time, like destruction.

This appreciation does not arrive immediately. It requires the distance of time and the integration of experience. But it is real, and it is significant. Every transition you manage successfully stands as a milestone and proof throughout your life that you can endure change, adapt to disruption, and emerge from forced transformations as someone greater than before.

The integration of change into a life is not a passive process. It requires the active work of aligning routines, beliefs, and self-understanding with the new reality. It embraces the lessons of the transition to reshape how we move through the world, rather than simply filing the experience away and resuming the previous patterns. Those who integrate change well do not simply survive their disruptions. They are transformed by them in ways that make subsequent changes, however difficult, navigable from a greater depth of resources. They become, over time, not people to whom change no longer happens, but people who have learned to meet it with wisdom that was not available to them before.

The Waterbed and the Bottom

Change is not just a mechanism of growth. It is a forced pilgrimage toward maturity one that most of us would not undertake voluntarily, because the destination requires passing through territory we would choose to avoid if the choice were entirely ours.

This is not just an idea to me; it is something I have lived, carrying a distinct significance and a precise place in my memory.

My journey into the most significant forced change began with a dream showing me my future. I also revealed what my beloved Harvey the place of my origins would become. I saw the dark clouds on the horizon. The decision to follow the dream into the military arrived early and a life of structure and discipline which I needed more than I knew.

Military service built something in me which made me better than I was. It also reinforced something that would take years more to fully see which was the illusion that I was in control. The military rewards control. It prizes it, cultivates it, makes it feel like the highest virtue. I came out of that season believing, more deeply than I had before I entered it, that the management of outcomes was not just possible but my responsibility.

Then the relationship ended, and the illusion cracked.

I did not understand at first what had actually broken. I told myself the story that most people tell when a relationship ends: this is about loss, about grief, about the specific absence of a specific person. And that was true, as far as it went. But beneath the grief lay something I was not yet willing to look at directly: the revelation that I had never had the control I thought I had, not over the relationship, the outcome, and most devastatingly, not over myself.

I was a control freak. I had always known this in some abstract sense, the way we know things about ourselves that we have not yet been forced to fully confront. The breakup made it concrete. I had built my emotional stability on the belief that it was my duty to manage the variables and outcomes of my life. And when the most important relationship in my life ended despite everything, I had done to manage it, the foundation of that belief gave way. Mental health professionals call this Identity Collapse.

What followed was a collapse I did not see coming.

I remember lying on my waterbed in the aftermath of the breakup with the relationship still raw, the grief still fresh and pounding, the disorientation of a life that had been reorganized around another person now confronting the fact that she left me alone. The waterbed, with its slow undulation, its quality of holding you while refusing to be still, became a strange and precise metaphor for everything I was feeling. I could not find solid ground. Every time I thought I had steadied myself, the surface shifted again beneath me.

I lay there and I wept. Not the controlled, manageable grief but the kind of weeping that takes over your body. A grief that comes from somewhere below the level of a conscious decision, from the place where what we feel is disconnected from what I tried to feel. I was not only sad but was hitting rock bottom.

And at the bottom, something became undeniable: I could not fix this under my own strength. The tools I had relied on the discipline, self-management, and the careful control of every variable within reach had failed me at the deepest level. I had less control over my own interior life, I realized in that moment, than I had ever had over anyone or anything external to me. The person I had been trying most desperately to manage was myself but incapable. I felt myself slipping further into the PIT, unable to stop my decline.

That moment on the waterbed was when I realized that I had lost control of my mind and emotions. It was too dramatic of entrance I would have scripted for myself, but the honest one of just lying alone, stripped of the illusion of control, finally pleading help I could not provide for myself.

I cried out to God not with eloquence but with desperation. Not with a theology of surrender but with the simple, raw acknowledgment that I had run out of myself. I woke up the next morning realizing that I needed to start walking trusting God by putting one foot in front of the other and walking towards the light which I could not see. In that darkness over the months and years that followed, something began to change. The transformation that the PIT made possible could not have begun any earlier, because the illusion of self-sufficiency had to be completely exhausted before the work could start.

It took years to fully accept what I had known about myself but been unable to change. The suppressed anger. The loneliness was masked by busyness and the performance of competence. The deep resistance to the vulnerability that change requires. These did not dissolve overnight. They were addressed slowly, honestly, in the daily discipline of a spiritual practice that was less about feeling better and more about becoming different.

As I have aged, I have become more adaptive to change, more accepting of its inevitability, and more resilient in its presence. This is not due to change becoming inherently less challenging, but rather because I have gained the wisdom in navigating transitions and growing from them. As a result, I am now able to approach future disruptions with preparedness rather than apprehension. I have learned to hold my plans with open hands. I have learned that the things I cannot control are often the very things through which the most important formation occurs.

I understand that challenges and setbacks are not interruptions to a story that was supposed to end differently, but as essential chapters that were still being written. When we live guided by wisdom, accept change as inevitable, let go of our urge to control every outcome, and trust the process even during difficult times, we reach places that sheer willpower and management could never take us.

The waterbed was not the lowest point of my life because of what I lost. It was the lowest point because of what was finally revealed. A revelation, however painful, is always the beginning of something.

A change will come and it is already coming. In the forms you have anticipated and in the forms you have not, in the moments you have prepared for and those you have not, through the doors you have chosen and through the walls you did not know could give way.

The question is not whether you will be changed. You will. The question is whether you will be transformed allowing change to do its full work, rather than spending your energy resisting a process that will unfold anyway.

The currents of life are inevitable. You do not have to fight it to survive it. You have to learn to navigate it with honest acceptance, creative adaptation, and the deep, sustaining trust that the river knows where it is going even when you cannot see the destination.

Change is not happening to you.
It is happening for you.

CHAPTER ELEVEN

The Solitary Path

Reclaiming Wholeness

Middle East

In 2012, I volunteered for an assignment in the Middle East with the U.S. Government. On paper, it was a career decision with more income, broader experience, a step away from the familiar. But beneath that practical rationale was something harder to name: a quiet, persistent need to find peace within myself.

I was carrying bitterness; I could not fully articulate and an unease that no external success seemed to touch. I felt spiritually depleted and restless, caught in the gap between the life I was living and the life I sensed was possible. Something needed to change, and I didn't know what. I only knew that I needed some distance from everything which seemed familiar. The life I had prayed for, longed for, and built around me was good, but I still felt unfulfilled.

When I arrived in Kuwait, the desert sand made the place look like another planet. Harsh, quiet, and unrelenting. Sandstorms blurred the horizon. The night air was filled with diesel smoke and the constant hum of hundreds of generators.

The first gift arrived unexpectedly, in a car enroute to Camp Arifjan.

My driver, a young man named Muhammad drove me from the airport to the military base. We talked for the length of that drive about our faith his in Islam and mine in Christianity with an ease that surprised me. He spoke about his relationship with Allah with directness and a sincerity that cut through every denominational boundary. He knew the creator as Allah, and I spoke of Jesus Christ.

Here, in a conversation with a stranger on a desert road, the same recognition arrived again: every human heart, regardless of the tradition that shaped it, is seeking the same connection. That simple exchange marked the beginning of my restoration. I was reminded that human conversations about the Divine are among the most powerful spiritual lessons available to us.

My work in quality assurance was demanding, and the environment was harsh and abrasive offering no cushion against the interior work that began almost immediately. It was as if the external barrenness had been arranged precisely to mirror my internal need for cleansing. I could not fill the silence with the usual distractions. I was left with myself.

I prayed daily not the structured, confident prayers of a man who knows what he is asking for, but the uncertain, reaching prayers of someone who has run out of answers hoping for another transformation. I asked God what this season meant. Instead of an immediate answer, I started listening more closely to things I had previously ignored or avoided.

Life in Kuwait tested my endurance in ways I had not anticipated. The heat was brutal, unrelenting in its intensity and leaving little room for comfort. The loneliness pressed close, a constant companion in the midst of unfamiliar surroundings. Each day was marked by the monotony of work and the sameness of routine, with little to distinguish one day from the next. The physical distance from everyone I loved only deepened the sense of isolation.

These were not the circumstances I would have chosen for a season of spiritual renewal. Yet, paradoxically, it was precisely these challenging conditions that made renewal possible. Stripped of distraction, I was left with the desert, the work at hand, my prayers, and the slow, unglamorous process of becoming honest with myself. The barrenness of the environment mirrored the interior work that was being asked of me, calling me toward a deeper honesty and acceptance within.

Then came the opportunity for reassignment to Bahrain. I did formally campaign for it, but I prayed and asked God for a path I needed to take to be selected over ten other quality assurance professionals. I made my case based on my construction experience building KFC, Pizza Hut, and Taco Bell restaurants for Yum-Yum corporation with my uncle Larry.

I prayed quietly and prepared carefully, trusting that if it was meant for me, the timing would confirm it. When the assignment was granted, I was selected over all the other seasoned quality professionals. Many who frequently made the rotations to the desert were frustrated when I was selected. The quality director said the choice was easy after reviewing my presentation. It felt less like professional development and more like a confirmation. It served a gentle reminder that faith and preparation must walk together, and that when they do, doors open where effort alone cannot.

Bahrain was different from the first breath. The island air carried life and possibility. The atmosphere was more open, diverse, and vibrant with the texture of human encounters. I discovered there and later in Oman that restoration is not always about withdrawal. Sometimes it is about rediscovering connections. Conversations with people from dozens of nations and backgrounds reminded me of the irreducible shared humanity beneath all the differences. A kind invitation to share camel milk in an Omani home. The laughter of strangers in a crowded flea market. Swimming in the Persian Gulf. A Russian band playing American songs in a foreign bar with an enthusiasm that made the distance between cultures feel absurd and wonderful. These small, unremarkable moments became sacred. They reawakened a gratitude I had not known I had lost.

And then came the news that stopped everything.

My uncle Larry had died by suicide. His final words to me "I love you" took on a weight and a depth I had not grasped when he said them. I sat with that grief in the middle of the desert, far from home and family, in a season that was supposed to be about my own restoration. I learned something in that grief that I could not have learned any other way: that restoration also means making peace with loss. That love and pain can coexist within the same truth, refining our spirit.

As my deployment ended, two Bangladeshi dining workers sought me out to thank me for my kindness toward them throughout the year. Their words touched me more than they could have known. They were confirmation of something I had come to understand slowly over those months: that when we heal internally, the light extends outward without effort or announcement. Restoration is never only personal. It radiates outwardly.

When I returned home, I carried with me a kind of quietness that felt both new and deeply soothing. This wasn't the emptiness of silence or the fatigue of weariness; rather, it was a peacefulness that came from being pared down to my core which was free of distractions, pretenses, and unnecessary layers and while spending time with the creator.

Through this process, I discovered that what remained was not only sufficient, but more than enough. The essential qualities revealed through solitude, challenges, and honest self-examination were all that was needed. This quietness, rooted in acceptance and clarity, marked the true culmination of my journey. It was the quiet of restoration, a peace that allowed me to be present with myself and others, grounded in the awareness that the essentials of life and spirit are more than adequate.

The Need for Restoration

Every journey of restoration begins with an honest recognition that something within has grown weary. The cycle of living, giving, and striving can leave us operating from a place of deficit, where the demands of life drain more than they replenish. When this goes unaddressed long enough, even our best intentions begin to falter. We give from an empty place and wonder why the giving feels hollow.

Restoration is not simply the repair of what has been damaged. It is the return to balance and the reconnection with a vitality and sacred rhythm that sustains one's wholeness. When we ignore the inner call for restoration, we drift from the wholeness that anchors us, losing touch with the peace that makes our presence in the world possible.

Recognizing this depletion is the first act of healing. It requires the willingness to stop performing wellness long enough to honestly assess the actual state of the interior life. This is harder than it sounds. Many of us have been trained by our culture, necessity, and legitimate demands of the people who depend on us to keep moving regardless of what is happening inside. The recognition that we need to stop, to withdraw, to tend to something that has been neglected can feel like failure. It is not. It is the most honest thing a depleted person can do.

Exhaustion is not failure. It is a sacred invitation.

The Pathway to Restoration

Once we have acknowledged the need for restoration, the work begins. This work is not passive, automatic, or something that happens simply because we have decided we want to do it. The pathway to restoration requires intention. The deliberate tending of the interior combined with the willingness to receive what we cannot manufacture through effort alone.

Restoration begins with the choice to treat our inner life with the same intentionality we bring to our outer responsibilities. This means nourishing the body through adequate rest, movement, and the kind of physical care that is easy to neglect when the demands of life feel more pressing. It means restoring the mind through reflection and the deliberate creation of space for quiet. It means tending the spirit through prayer, gratitude, and the practices that open us to something larger than our own understanding.

At the foundation of all of this is self-love, which is genuinely not performed. Without compassion for our own imperfections and honest acceptance of our humanity, restoration cannot fully unfold. Loving ourselves means extending to ourselves the same patience we would offer to someone we cared for deeply: the permission to be tired, to be unfinished, to be in process. It means forgiving what has been left undone without using the undone as evidence of fundamental inadequacy.

Self-love isn't self-indulgence; it builds inner stability, enabling service, growth, and authentic connection with others. You cannot give from a place of emptiness. You cannot sustain generosity from a foundation of self-contempt. Restoration requires first filling what has been emptied.

Solitude as Preparation, Not Isolation

The solitary path of this chapter's title is not the same as isolation. Isolation is the withdrawal that comes from pain, which is the pulling away from connection that has become too costly or threatening. Solitude is different. It is the intentional withdrawal into stillness for the purpose of restoration. It presents the choice to step back from the noise of ordinary life long enough to hear what has been drowned out by it.

Solitude requires courage. Our culture is deeply uncomfortable with stillness. We fill every available moment with external inputs some digital, social, and professional. The person who chooses solitude for restoration makes a conscious decision to pause and acknowledge their depletion. Rather than pushing past exhaustion or masking it with constant activity, they allow themselves to fully experience the emptiness which has accumulated. This act is not passive; it is a deliberate recognition that restoration cannot begin until the depth of depletion is honestly felt and accepted. Only then does the process of rebuilding truly commence, grounded in the awareness of what needs to be restored.

What the desert of Kuwait taught me was that solitude strips away the unnecessary with a thoroughness that comfort never demands. In the absence of distraction, what remains is the present unresolved grief, unnamed bitterness, the quiet longing for something more aligned. These are not comfortable companions. But they are honest ones. And honesty, encountered with patience, is always the beginning of something.

Openness to the Unexpected

Restoration may not arrive in the form we would have designated. The conversation we needed came from a stranger on a desert road. The reassignment that opened new life came through a plan and quiet faith. The grief that deepened compassion arrived as loss, not gift. The gratitude that was reawakened came through camel milk in an Omani home and a Russian band playing American songs.

This is the character of restoration: it uses what is available rather than what we would have chosen. It works through the ordinary and the unexpected rather than through the dramatic and the planned. The person who insists that restoration arrives in a particular form, on a particular schedule, through a particular means, will miss most of what is being offered. The posture that receives restoration most fully is openness and the willingness to be surprised and moved by what we did not anticipate. Finding sacredness in what presents itself rather than in what we sought.

The Fruits of Restoration

The culmination of the solitary path is not the end of striving. It is the beginning of balance and a shift in how we understand and inhabit time, purpose, and growth. The person restored is not the same as the person who entered the season of depletion. As the journey of restoration unfolds, it becomes clear that the process is not simply about regaining what was lost. Something new has been added to oneself with depth and clarity, fostering a renewed sense of presence that was forged through solitude and honest self-examination. At the same time, something has also been released.

The burdens, excesses, and distractions that no longer serve are allowed to fall away, leaving space for what is essential. This dual movement, the gaining of what is vital and the letting go of what is unnecessary marks the transformation that restoration brings. It is through this balance of receiving and releasing that wholeness begins to emerge, anchoring the person in a peace that is both restorative and sustaining.

The most immediate fruit of restoration is experiencing inner peace, not the absence of difficulty or challenge, but the capacity to remain anchored in the presence of both. This is the peace that the desert, for all its harshness, eventually delivered: not a peace that depended on the circumstances becoming comfortable, but a peace that persisted within and through them.

Alongside peace comes a renewal of creative energy, the return of curiosity, engagement, and the desire to build, contribute, and connect. Depletion silences these impulses. Restoration revives them. The person who has rested and allowed the restoration to process its full work returns to engagement with the vitality of life.

Restoration Radiates

One of the discoveries of this season that I did not anticipate was that restoration is never only personal. When we heal internally, the light extends outward without conscious effort. The two Bangladeshi workers followed me out of a building to thank me as my deployment was ending. They were responding to my outward presence of kindness. A quality that had been restored, over the course of that year, through prayer and solitude, while grieving showing up wherever I was needed.

This is how restoration contributes to the world: not through grand gestures, but through the changed quality of our ordinary presence. The restored person sees others more clearly, listens more fully, gives more genuinely, because they are giving from a place that has been replenished rather than depleted. Restoration, undertaken for the sake of oneself, ultimately becomes a gift to everyone the restored person touches.

Restoration teaches that wholeness doesn't mean perfection or being free from wounds, weaknesses, or struggles. It is the capacity to stand in the middle of life's unpredictability and remain anchored. To be present without being consumed. To be whole is to carry the full spectrum of human life: its grief and its beauty, its losses and its moments of breakthrough.

Wholeness allows us to carry these experiences without letting any one of them define or undo us. It is a state where we can acknowledge pain and celebrate joy, all the while remaining resilient and intact, while not collapsing under the weight of what life brings.

Reclaiming wholeness is not a destination. It is a rhythm and a balance between effort and surrender, solitude and connection, striving and rest. The solitary path does not end with a single season of restoration. It becomes, over time, a way of moving through the world: attentive to the inner life, responsive to the invitation of stillness, trusting that the pauses are never wasted, and that the Divine's presence was there through it all.

We were never alone in this. We only need to be quiet enough to hear it.

Solitude is not emptiness.
It is a place where we make time to heal.

CHAPTER TWELVE

A Structured Approach Through Depression

The Invitation Cycle

Treatment Resistant Depression

There is a particular kind of despair that forms when you've tried everything you were told would work and you're still not okay. You did the responsible things. You showed up to appointments. You took the medication. You sat through therapy even when you felt numb. You changed your diet, routine, mindset, and yet the darkness stayed. You prayed and tried again.

This chapter is for the person who has begun to wonder, quietly and painfully, *"What if I'm the exception?"*

Treatment-Resistant Depression (TRD) is not a character flaw. It is not proof that you didn't try hard or believe hard enough. TRD is what we call depression that does not respond to treatment the way we expect it to respond even when a person has made honest efforts to heal. And that reality can be terrifying, because it doesn't just challenge your mood; it challenges your hope.

After repeated disappointment, the mind starts to form a dangerous conclusion: *Nothing will work. Nothing will change. This is permanent.*

But what if that conclusion is not truth... only exhaustion talking?

Emerging from depression especially TRD often requires a different approach than simply "trying harder." It requires learning to recognize the patterns that keep the mind trapped, the signals the body has been sending for years, and the unseen ways the spirit has been carrying more than it was designed to hold alone. TRD is complex.

It can involve biology, trauma, chronic stress, nervous system dysregulation, sleep disruption, inflammation, grief, and hundreds of quiet burdens that compound over time. That means the pathway forward is rarely one single fix. It's usually a map made of small, consistent steps that restore stability, agency, and the ability to feel meaning again.

In this chapter, we're going to name what TRD is and what it is not. We'll examine why some people don't respond to standard approaches for depression, and it is important to recognize that a lack of response does not mean a person is beyond help. The experience of not improving with typical approaches can be deeply discouraging, but it does not define a person's capacity for healing.

Healing often begins with a shift in perspective: rather than viewing the mind as an adversary, it can be more helpful to see symptoms as meaningful signals. These symptoms are not signs of failure; instead, they offer information about what the mind and body might need. By moving away from self-blame and the idea that non-response is a personal defect, there is room to approach depression with greater compassion and curiosity.

This mindset allows for the exploration of new strategies and the recognition that persistent symptoms may be pointing toward underlying factors which require attention. Ultimately, the journey toward healing becomes less about fighting against oneself and more about listening, understanding, and responding with care to the messages the mind and body are sending.

We will also explore practical, grounded next steps in both clinical and non-clinical approaches without shame, hype, and without pretending there's a shortcut.

If you've been living in the PIT for a long time, let this be your first reminder: A Place in Time is not the same as a permanent identity. The fog may have reduced visibility, but the path has not disappeared. And even if you cannot feel hope right now, you can still move toward one intentional choice at a time.

Treatment-Resistant Depression (TRD) is one of the most misunderstood experiences in mental health because from the outside it can look like a person is "not doing enough," when they have often done more than most people realize.

They have tried medication. They have tried therapy. They have tried routines, supplements, exercise, prayer, discipline, and gratitude. They have tried to outwork the darkness. And still, the symptoms remain.

TRD is not a moral failure. It is not a lack of effort. It is not proof that someone doesn't want to get better.

What Is Treatment-Resistant Depression?

Treatment-Resistant Depression, often referred to as TRD, is the term clinicians use when depression does not respond adequately to standard first-line treatments. This means that even after engaging with approaches like "Talk Therapy" and Cognitive Behavior Therapy (CBT), and even when those treatments have been given a fair and appropriate trial, the depressive symptoms persist.

In other words, TRD describes the experience of having followed recommended care by attending therapy sessions, participating in evidence-based methods, and giving these options the time and effort they require but recognizing improvement. This can be deeply discouraging, as it may feel like the usual roads to recovery are not working, even when one has committed fully to the process.

In plain terms, TRD often means: *You did what you were told should help... and you're still stuck.*

That reality creates a specific kind of suffering not only the pain of depression, but the pain of repeated disappointment. Over time, the mind begins forming a conclusion that feels logical: Nothing works for me.I am an exception.This is permanent.

The Voice of Exhaustion

It is important to understand the belief that thinking "Nothing will work. Nothing will change. This is permanent" is not necessarily the truth.

More often, it is the voice of exhaustion speaking, attempting to shield you from hope because hope has felt too costly to pursue. Exhaustion can distort perceptions and make it feel as if progress is impossible, but this feeling is not a definitive reflection of reality. Instead, it is a response to repeated disappointment and fatigue, and recognizing this distinction can be the first step toward a more compassionate approach to your experience.

Why Understanding Treatment-Resistant Depression Matters

Recognizing the importance of understanding Treatment-Resistant Depression (TRD) is crucial. When depression continues despite previous efforts, it typically signals there are some core challenges present. Identifying which challenge is at play helps guide the next steps toward recovery and provides clarity about the path forward.

Sometimes, persistent depression indicates that the current treatment strategy needs to be revised. This might mean expanding the methods used, adapting the plan to better suit the individual's unique biology, or aligning interventions more closely with their history. The standard approaches may not be enough, and a tailored response is often necessary to address the complexity of TRD.

In other situations, depression is sustained by unrecognized or unaddressed factors. These underlying drivers quietly feed the condition, keeping the system locked in familiar, unproductive patterns. Without identifying and responding to these hidden contributors, progress remains elusive, and symptoms persist despite best efforts.

Understanding which of these challenges is present can be the turning point for moving out of the cycle of being stuck. By examining which hidden drivers it becomes possible to break through the patterns that keep depression entrenched, offering a path forward.

Treatment-Resistant Depression (TRD) is rarely the result of a single, isolated issue. Instead, it often emerges as a complex web of interconnected factors. These can include biological influences, ongoing strain on the nervous system, the lingering effects of trauma, disruptions in sleep patterns, and the presence of chronic stress. Grief, inflammation, social isolation, a sense of identity collapse, or unresolved emotional pain can all play significant roles as well.

This tangled web means that the mind may find itself repeatedly circling through the same pain points, unable to settle because it has not yet discovered a place of safety or resolution. TRD, therefore, is not simply a matter of a single failed treatment or a missed step; it reflects an intricate interplay of challenges that require careful, compassionate, and multifaceted response.

The goal of this chapter is not to offer a simple answer. The goal is to give you something more valuable:

A better interpretation of what persistent depression may be signaling, and a more grounded map of what may be emerging. Because when you stop blaming yourself for not responding, you can finally begin asking the questions that are needed:

What is sustaining this depression?

What have we not tried yet or possibly not tried in the right order?

What does my mind keep signaling through exhaustion, numbness, and despair?

What would it look like to respond with a comprehensive strategy?

TRD is not the end of the story, but it does require a different kind of approach one that respects complexity and rebuilds hope through the smallest reliable steps.

When depression becomes treatment-resistant, one of the most dangerous conclusions the mind can reach is this: "*Nothing works, so nothing matters.*"

That belief doesn't just deepen sadness; it deepens helplessness. And helplessness is where the PIT becomes permanent in a person's imagination.

This is why Treatment-Resistant Depression (TRD) often calls for more than simply trying yet another technique. What is truly needed is a different relationship with how you approach your thoughts and responses.

Even during persistent symptoms where something triggers you, a thought spirals out of control, emotions build, and your mind instinctively begins searching for a way out. While TRD may be ongoing, the cycle of reaction and response is still at work. If this cycle continues to operate, there remains an entry point for changing how you intervene by shifting your experience incrementally.

That entry point is the Invitation Cycle™.

The Invitation Cycle™: A Framework for Regaining Agency

The Invitation Cycle™ does not serve as a substitute for clinical care. Instead, it offers a practical framework designed to help individuals reclaim a sense of agency during moments of mental distress.

This approach is valuable when the mind begins to loop, exhaustion intensifies, intrusive thoughts re-emerge, or fear of one's own thoughts creates the urge to withdraw.

By providing structure and guidance, the Invitation Cycle™ empowers individuals to respond thoughtfully to these challenging mental states.

Rather than simply reacting or shutting down, it encourages intentional engagement, creating space for choice and self-compassion even in the midst of overwhelming symptoms.

The cycle is meant to be used alongside professional support, serving as a complement to clinical interventions and a tool for building resilience in everyday life.

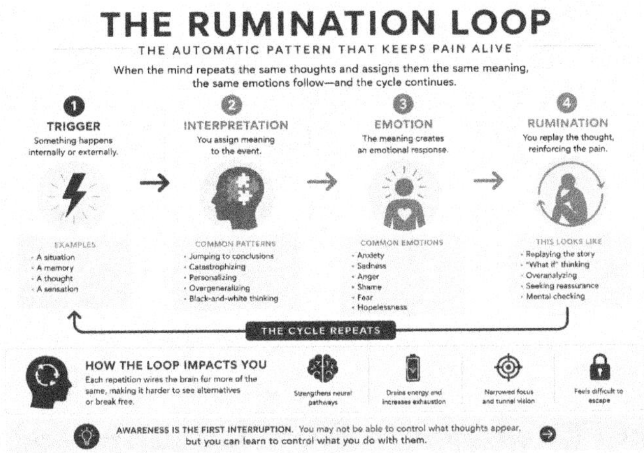

TRD causes people to wait for feelings before acting, but healing starts not with feelings, but with intentional action.

Four Phases

Interrupt

Treatment-Resistant Depression (TRD) often leaves the mind feeling out of control, like a runaway train which cannot be stopped. In these moments, the step of "***Interrupt***" becomes crucial. Instead of engaging in an argument with the troubling thought or trying to reason your way out, Interrupt is intentionally breaking the momentum. This break does not require a grand gesture; it simply means to pause, creating a momentary gap in the escalation.

By making space in the mental process, Interrupt allows you to step back from the automatic cycle. This space is not just an absence; it is where possibility begins. When you gain even a few inches of emotional or cognitive distance, you unlock the potential for choice. This act of interrupting the cycle is the first step toward regaining agency, offering a brief respite that makes intentional response possible.

Interpret

In the Invitation Cycle™, the step of ***Interpret*** is about shifting from judgment to curiosity. Instead of accepting troubling thoughts as absolute truths or final verdicts, you begin to treat them as signals and messages from your mind that carry information about your internal state. This step invites you to pause and ask important questions: *What is this moment* *revealing?* What triggered this response? What story has my mind created around this experience? What emotion is beginning to surface? These are conversations of the mind.

By asking these questions, you move away from the tendency to let depression define your reality and instead start to understand what your mind is communicating. This approach is crucial in Treatment-Resistant Depression (TRD), where depression often disguises actual needs as conclusions, making it easy to believe that the feeling is the end of the story. Through interpretation, you uncover what your system truly requires at this moment, whether it is rest, support, connection, or another form of care. This step helps you respond thoughtfully, rather than reactively, breaking the cycle of despair by seeing thoughts as signals which can guide you toward healing.

Integrate

Integration is the step where the insights gained from interpreting your thoughts and emotions are transformed into care and practical action. This process involves connecting what you have observed within yourself such as the need for rest, boundaries, connection, grief, support, medical evaluation, trauma work, or spiritual grounding to the areas that require attention. Integration is not about finding a quick fix or solution; instead, it is about creating alignment between your internal experiences and your responses. Through integration, you learn to treat your inner world with wisdom, offering compassion and support rather than punishment or neglect. By aligning your actions with what your mind and body are signaling, you foster a more nurturing and resilient relationship with yourself, paving the way for healing and growth during persistent symptoms.

Intentionally Choose

The step of ***Intentionally Choose*** is where you reclaim a sense of agency, even during Treatment-Resistant Depression. This is not about making a sweeping, life-changing decision. Instead, it is about taking a single, manageable action one that is accessible and realistic in the moment. This could be something as simple as making a phone call, taking a short walk, preparing and eating a meal, writing a few lines in a journal, scheduling or attending a therapy appointment, saying a brief prayer, changing your environment, or setting a small boundary.

The key is that the chosen action is "aligned." Alignment does not mean you will necessarily feel good about it at the moment. Rather, it means the action moves you in the direction of stability, care, and support, rather than allowing you to slip further into isolation or despair. Each small, intentional choice is a step away from helplessness, reinforcing your ability to respond to your experience with purpose, even when relief feels distant. These choices, repeated over time, create momentum and help anchor you to the present, offering a path forward, one step at a time.

For someone living with TRD, this is the first important reassurance: *You may not be able to control what thoughts appear, but you can learn to control what you do with them.*

And that's why the Invitation Cycle™ belongs in this chapter. Because when a person has tried everything and still feels stuck, what they need most is not another reason to feel hopeless. They need a way to respond in real time when the mind begins to spiral. Waiting is not a strategy but responding with intention is.

And if you're reading this from within the PIT, let this be your closing truth: *You are not failing because you're still fighting. You are not weak because you are exhausted. You are not beyond reach.*

TRD is not the end of your story.

The Invitation Cycle™ is simply the next faithful step

This chapter does not minimize depression's severity. It takes the darkness seriously on clinical, emotional, and spiritual levels. And within that seriousness, the Invitation Cycle is a structured-approach for emerging from depression. Anyone can choose to let go of what can't be controlled while taking responsibility for those things that can.

The PIT is a state of being, not a permanent address.

My Journey

There was a day when I felt the edges of myself fraying. Sleepless nights. No appetite. Thoughts racing in circles too loud and too fast to follow. I walked into the clinic, answered the questions, and sat across from a psychologist who handed me a prescription. At the door, I paused. I chose not to fill it.

I want to be careful here: that choice was mine, shaped by my faith, and by my conviction about what my particular situation required. But medication is not the enemy of faith. For many people, it isn't just helpful; but rather essential. There is no virtue in unnecessary suffering, and getting clinical support is not a spiritual failure.

What I wanted most was understanding. I needed language for what was happening to me because the shift felt impossible to explain. One day I seemed fine, and then suddenly my world collapsed. It wasn't just sadness. It was as if my confidence, stability, and sense of self caved overnight.

This sudden and profound change left me searching for a way to express the turmoil within. The loss went deeper than fleeting emotion; it affected the very foundation of my identity. I struggled to describe how my inner world had shifted so dramatically, making it feel as though the core of who I was had vanished without warning. The need for understanding and language became essential, providing a sense of clarity and dignity amid confusion, pain, and suffering.

In the course of thirty years of journaling, writing, and researching this book, I found a term that finally gave shape to that experience: Identity Collapse. The moment I encountered it, something clicked. It didn't take away the pain, but it gave it a name.

It offered a frame for what I had been living through. A way to understand how your entire life can change the inner environment in a single moment.

So, I turned towards God not as a theological position, but as a practical, daily decision. I began spending my lunch breaks in my truck, listening to hopeful messages from pastors like Chuck Smith, Charles Stanley, and Charles Swindoll letting their words reach me where logic no longer could.

They steadied me enough to help get me through the day. But I remained frozen. I kept praying, showing up, and holding on.

The breakthrough arrived not as a revelation but as an admission: I was not running my life. My fear was. I saw, for the first time with clarity, how my pain had become an anchor keeping me safe from my own healing. I had been clinging to the anguish as though releasing it meant releasing the proof that I was suffering. The anchor that had once kept me from falling apart was now keeping me from coming back together.

As I sat with that truth, I realized no one was coming to rescue me from the PIT, and I had to take part in my own healing. The climb out required only something I could do.

From that point, I began practicing the two things that recovery requires:

Rather than trying to master the illusion of controlling depression, I discovered that forcing things simply wasn't effective. What truly mattered was gaining mastery over aspects that were within my control: my sleep routines, thought processes, staying present in each moment, and how I reacted when rumination threatened to take over. At the same time, I realized it was unrealistic to expect that I could control other people's decisions or those outcomes.

I learned something painfully and important while performing bereavement group sessions that the darkest thoughts were rarely proof that someone really wanted life to end. More often it was evidence of the **Exhaustion Paradox** that they didn't want death; I also wanted *relief*. I also wanted the exhausting internal battle to stop the rumination loop of intrusive thoughts that returned like echoes creating uncertainty affecting my mental health. When I finally understood it, the shame loosened. I stopped treating those thoughts as a verdict and started treating them as a signal that my system was overloaded; something needs attention.

That understanding provided a practical path forward. I started applying elements of the Invitation Cycle™ to my daily life rather than just treating it as a theory. Whenever I sensed the loop beginning, I would **interrupt** it. Then, I'd **interpret** what underlying feelings like tiredness, sadness, loneliness, or fear conveyed. By **integrating** these insights, I adjusted my routines and support systems instead of being hard on myself for continued struggles. Finally, I would **intentionally choose** my next step: taking one small action to head toward stability, rather than retreat further into isolation.

I built simple, durable routines that could carry me when my emotions could not. I kept a short journal that measured progress in inches rather than miles, because TRD rarely heals through dramatic breakthroughs; it heals through the quiet accumulation of evidence that change is still possible. And I asked God to meet me in the next breath instead of the next decade, because when exhaustion reaches that depth, grace must come close enough to breathe.

The light returned gently, like morning filtering through the window blinds after a rainy night. The light came back to my life, not in an overwhelming or sudden moment, but through a gradual, unwavering presence that was new to me. There was no single dramatic event that marked my transformation. Instead, change unfolded gently, one decision at a time, as I consistently made small choices toward health. This process stretched over days, months, and years, each step reinforcing my movement toward stability.

Through this journey, I learned that true freedom is not defined by the disappearance of sorrow. Rather, freedom is found when sorrow no longer has the authority to define my identity. I became able to acknowledge pain without letting it dictate who I am or how I move forward.

I rediscovered contentment in being myself not flawlessly or without continual work. Still, my happiness feels real and lasting, anchored in something that outside events can shake but not remove. Alongside that, my purpose became clear: to share honestly about the struggle and the journey beyond it, and to offer what I've discovered to others who may be seeking answers.

This breakthrough is not something I celebrate as an achievement, but something I carry as a solemn way of living marked by gratitude, attentiveness, and a willingness to keep moving forward. The practices that sustained me remain coupled with ongoing conversations with God that has neither faded nor ended.

The world had not changed. I did. And that has made my world and place within it more peaceable.

The darkness of the PIT is real. This chapter has not argued otherwise. But it is not total, and it is not permanent, and it does not have the final word about who you are or what remains possible for you.

The exit is not found by waiting for the darkness to lift on its own. It is found by making the decision imperfect, uncertain, taken in the presence of fear rather than in its absence to begin the climb. One small, faithful, specific action at a time.

With whatever support is available. Sustained by the conviction that the same force that has been present through every season of this journey is present in this one too, and that the door that feels invisible from inside is nevertheless there, and when it opens you will be ready.

The PIT is not your prison. You are free to open the door when you are ready to leave.

InvitationCycle.co
m

PART FOUR

Suicidal Thoughts

There is a massive, lethal myth surrounding self-destruction that we must dismantle right now: the idea that suicide is always a sudden, dramatic, and impulsive leap off a visible ledge. We are conditioned to look only for the loud, catastrophic moments of crisis, entirely missing the far more common, stealthy reality.

The truth is that suicide often begins as a slow, systemic mindset shift a quiet, daily manipulation where a person gradually signs off on their own exit through small, incremental choices. It is the patient who reaches for a cigarette immediately after a grueling cancer treatment; it is the individual who uses alcohol to systematically erode their relationships, career, and their health; it is the passive, slow-motion surrender of a person who has decided to let themselves bleed out in the dark.

The gradual manipulation of the exit

This profound insight is not born from academic theory; it is forged from my frontline crisis intervention experience , and the devastating, unvarnished history of the people I loved and lost. I watched this slow, rationalized retreat destroy my uncle as the financial wreckage of 2008 quietly eroded his business until the weight became too much to bear.

I saw it in my neighbor, whose uncontrollable addiction and substance abuse systematically dismantled the beautiful life he could have lived. And I felt the agonizing limits of intervention with my cousin who quietly slipped away into the darkness after a hidden, failed attempt. I saw it with a coworker sacrificed his time and family consumed with playing video games for entertainment and a retreat from a stressful day.

None of these exits truly happened in a single day; they were the final events of a long, invisible war of attrition where the mind slowly rationalized that its presence no longer mattered. We must watch out for passive suicide to expose exactly how the mind manipulates reality. Under extreme emotional pressure, your internal sensors malfunction, and the mind begins to frame self-sabotage not as destruction, but as a comforting form of relief.

It whispers that giving up in increments is safer than fighting, that you are protecting others by slowly erasing yourself, or that a destructive lifestyle is just a harmless coping mechanism. This is a false report. To halt this slow bleed before it transforms into a final, irreversible event, one must erect an absolute defensive barrier.

One must look honestly at their daily habits to identify what is quietly sabotaging your quest for life. If this is applicable to you means you are still breathing, and that part of you wants to live brought you to this page.

Stand down from the slow exit, reject the notion of the gradual ending, and choose to stay with purpose.

Reflection Questions:

In what areas of my life have I slowly stopped choosing life not through one dramatic decision, but through repeated habits, compromises, or neglect?

What destructive behavior have I justified as "coping" or "surviving" that, if I am completely honest, is gradually taking me farther away from my purpose?

If someone who loved me observed my daily choices over the past year, would they conclude that I am intentionally building a meaningful life or quietly preparing to leave it?

If today became the moment I rejected every form of a slow exit, what single decision would demonstrate to choose life, purpose, and hope instead of gradual surrender?

CHAPTER THIRTEEN

Climbing Your Mountain

The Ascent to Purpose

Preparing for the Climb

Every journey through darkness is preparation for a climb.

In the PIT, we are confronted by depression, loss, seasons of unwanted change, and the painful interior work of transformation. Yet the PIT was never only a place of suffering; it was also a place of preparation. The climb requires first learning how to rise out of the PIT itself and then continuing upward toward the mountain's summit.

The person who has endured the previous chapters of this journey and done the honest work there has been developing, often without realizing it, the very capacities the ascent demands: resilience forged through suffering, patience refined by waiting, self-knowledge born from the stripping away of comforting illusions, and a faith tested deeply enough to be trusted on the climb ahead.

The mountain is not a metaphor for an easy life finally attained. It is a metaphor for pursuit itself—the ongoing, demanding, and deeply rewarding work of becoming who you were made to be and doing what you were made to do. The summit is not the end of the journey. It is, as anyone who has stood upon a mountaintop eventually discovers, simply the vantage point from which new mountains come into view.

This chapter is about the ascent: the preparation it demands, endurance required to continue climbing, and the perspective revealed from higher ground about the journey that made the climb possible.

The purpose for the climb begins not on the trail but in the quiet, unglamorous work of honest self-assessment. No one ascends a significant mountain without preparation. One who attempts it unprepared either will turn back early or not return at all. The inner preparation required for a purpose-driven life is similar to the preparation a climber brings before the climb begins.

Before the ascent can begin, there must first be a season of preparation. This is the ground-level work of honest internal conversation which demands both courage and stillness to endure. What do I truly believe about myself? Why am I making this climb, and how will I confront the voices I have carried for too long? What chapter of my life has ended, and what will the next season require of me that the last one never did? These are not ordinary questions. They are the questions that prepare a person for the ascent.

The recognition of a new chapter dawning is not merely a pleasant metaphor. Recognizing the start of a new chapter often comes with a distinct and sometimes unsettling realization: the story that once defined you no longer feels true. As you move forward, it becomes necessary to let go of that old narrative, understanding that its purpose was to guide you through a time that has now passed. Releasing this former identity is not always comfortable, but it creates space for a new sense of self, one that aligns with who you are becoming because of everything you have experienced and realize about yourself.

This recognition carries both grief and possibility: the grief of leaving behind what is familiar, even when the familiar was painful, and the possibility of a life more deeply aligned with who you are becoming.

This beginning is marked by a crucial shift: the movement from passive wishing to active decision. Not the vague hope for a better life, but concrete choices made in the conditions of ordinary life that signal a commitment to a new direction. These initial choices become the foundation of a firm decision representing the first footholds of the ascent. They matter not because they are dramatic, but because they are necessary.

Your climb begins by turning the page. The old narrative has served its purpose. The decisions you make start this new chapter.

The Inner Forge

The ascent demands a mind prepared for its conditions. Not a mind without fear or doubt but a mind that has been deliberately strengthened to carry its weight without being collapsed by it. Building a belief in yourself is the foundation.

True confidence is not the fragile kind that relies on the approval or recognition of others. Instead, it is a deep, unwavering sense of your own worth and ability. This settled, quiet assurance remains intact even when external circumstances are unfavorable, because it is grounded in something far more substantial than changing conditions.

This kind of self-belief does not come from positive thinking, repeated affirmations, or emotional optimism. It is a conviction rooted in inner independence rather than external validation. It is earned through the accumulation of honest self-knowledge, evidence of survival, and the recognition that the capacities you required at each stage of the journey were available when you needed them.

Eliminating the weight of mental toxicity that burdens the climb is essential. No climber reaches higher ground while carrying what slowly weakens their strength or clouds their judgment. The negative self-talk and limiting beliefs formed before you possessed the wisdom to question them can be released. The resentment and bitterness that have consumed energy for years while producing nothing of value in return are too heavy to carry. A climber sheds unnecessary weight before beginning the ascent. The same discipline applies here: examining what occupies the mind and developing the willingness to finally set down what was never meant to be carried this far.

The ascent to purpose is not a sprint but is coupled with patience. There will be stretches that feel like no progress is being made where the terrain is difficult; the summit is invisible, and the temptation to give up. Developing the mental endurance to continue moving through these stretches while maintaining focus on the goal is not a minor skill but a commitment.

The Life Preserver

I never had trouble believing in myself until I began to love and sacrifice more than I had to give. I learned when you love someone deeply, it's easy to extend ourselves by trusting from a vulnerable and honest place using our deepest reserves of care and commitment. This is not weakness but, the very nature of love.

I learned through my own suffering a truth that has shaped everything I have come to understand about the ascent since: the deepest and most complete form of surrender the kind that places your entire sense of worth, identity, and security into another person's hands was never meant to belong to another human being. It belongs to God alone.

My pain came from misplaced trust, a fundamental truth, during the journey upward. Surrendering in the deepest, most complete way by unintentionally handing over your entire sense of worth and security to another person is a big mistake. This level of surrender is not meant for another human being. It is a giving over that should be reserved for God alone. When you entrust your core identity and safety to someone else, you risk losing the very foundation needed for the climb. That lesson, I learned the hard way which has become a guiding principle for how I understand and approach life.

No human being is built to carry the weight of another human being who is an adult. And when we ask them to, we set both ourselves up for a collapse that neither intended. Giving more than we should isn't wise because we pour out more than we can sustain and more than the relationship can hold, weakening the very fortitude the ascent requires. We drain the reservoir, and a depleted climber on a difficult mountain is in real danger.

Enduring emotional hardship is essential to rising above adversity. It is the life preserver. It is the crevice clip that tethers a climber to the mountain face when the wind picks up and the footing becomes uncertain. Without it, the risk of a fatal fall is not hypothetical. It is the direct, predictable consequence of ascending without adequate protection.

There are things we should never give away, because in giving them we are placing absolute faith in another human being to safeguard, protect, and reciprocate which is God's role and responsibility. Our sense of worth is one of them, and our spiritual center is another. These are not selfish reservations; they represent the responsible stewardship of what makes the rest of our giving possible and sustainable.

The person who gives away their life preserver does not simply feel sad. They find themselves shielded in low self-esteem, trapped by negative emotions, and unable to climb because the equipment was given to someone who was never meant to carry it. Reclaiming that equipment is among the first acts in preparation for the ascent.

God has taught me, through repeated and sometimes painful experiences, the importance of climbing your own mountain. This does not mean climbing in isolation, refusing companionship, or declining the encouragement and support of others. A sense of community and mentorship matters. The presence of people who believe in your capacity when you have temporarily lost access to that belief yourself matters enormously.

The climb itself the actual, interior work of ascending toward your purpose is yours alone. No one else can do it for you. While relationships may offer love and support, they cannot replace the unique, personal effort where only you can commit. Waiting for ideal circumstances, the perfect companion, or the optimal level of support before starting the ascent leads only to an indefinite delay. The reality is that conditions will never be perfectly aligned. The journey must begin with what is present now, not what might be possible in the future. The first steps must be taken amid the circumstances you currently face, relying on your own resolve to advancing toward your purpose.

You can seek encouragement, but the climb is yours alone.

The Mountains of Purpose

Life is not defined by a single mountain to climb, but by an entire range of mountains stretching across a lifetime. Each summit, once reached, becomes a vantage point from which the next challenge comes into view. With every ascent, new heights are revealed, each requiring its own preparation, its own endurance, and its own particular form of courage.

This ongoing journey means that growth and purpose are not achieved in a single moment of triumph, but are continually forged as you move from one mountain to another. Every ascent demands readiness and resilience, and every summit reached equips you with the perspective and strength needed for what comes next. The process is ongoing: with each climb, you discover more about yourself and the path you are meant to follow.

After you reach one summit, you see others in the distance that you must eventually climb. This is not discouraging news. It is an accurate description of a life lived with genuine purpose and ongoing growth.

The mountains are formed by your dreams, aspirations, and the particular texture of your life experiences. Each person's range is unique. The mountains before you are not the same as the mountains before anyone else, because they have been shaped by a specific history, and a set of gifts and wounds, uniquely belonging to no one but you.

The mountain tests your inner truth and resolve in ways that flat terrain never could. It reveals your true beliefs about yourself, not what you claim or show others, but what hardship exposes at your core. This is not comfortable. It is necessary. You do not discover what you are made of in the easy seasons. You discover it on the face of the mountain, when the way is hard and the summit is not yet visible and continuing requires something you are not sure you have.

You learn to believe in yourself by the specific act of continuing. Not by thinking your way into belief, but by moving and taking the next steps, finding that it was possible. Belief built this way has a durability that no affirmation can produce. It is the accumulation of evidence, gathered in your own body and experiences, that you are capable of more than the voices of inner critic.

The wrong path matters, too. Every climber takes them. The descent back to a safe position after a route that did not work is not failure. It is information, and it is the origin of a better route. Each setback on the ascent carries a lesson that the summit itself could not have taught about the terrain, your own capacities and limitations, and the difference between the approach that looks promising and the one that doesn't.

One of the most important skills of the ascent is the capacity to transform negative energy into forward momentum. The anger, grief, and frustration of the long journey through the PIT are not liabilities to be suppressed. They are fuel, to be channeled rather than vented. The person who has suffered and processed that suffering in a positive way carries a motivational energy that comfort never generates.

One of the strongest motivations for continuing the ascent comes from a deep awareness of what you are climbing away from. This clarity about the alternative and the cost of remaining where you were serves as a powerful force, propelling you upward even when the journey is difficult. The knowledge of what it would mean to stay stuck, to remain in the PIT or to settle for less than your purpose, is not just a random thought but a conscious driver. It keeps the climb purposeful and focused.

This understanding becomes an anchor during challenging moments, reminding you that the struggle of the ascent is preferable to the pain of standing still. The memory of previous hardship, the limitations of the old terrain, and the consequences of not moving forward become fuel. They infuse each step with intention and resolve, making the effort to rise not just about reaching a new summit, but about refusing to return to the place you once were.

It is this conscious awareness of knowing exactly what you are leaving behind and the costs to stay there provides some of the most enduring energy for the journey. It transforms the climb from a vague aspiration into a deliberate act of self-rescue and growth. In this way, the ascent is not only about reaching for something higher, but also about honoring the commitment to never return to what you have already outgrown.

It does not pretend the pain was not real or that the losses did not matter. It simply refuses to let suffering become the final destination. Instead, it directs the energy contained within that pain upward toward building, creating, healing, and contributing to life recognizing that the suffering itself was part of the journey in preparation for the climb.

The summit does not end the journey, but it gives you something that the climbing could not, which is the view. The perspective that comes from having ascended from having done the work, endured the difficulty, and arrived at a higher place is not available from the base of the mountain. You cannot fully see the terrain you have traveled until you rise above it.

The summit enshrines you with inner strength and wisdom that could not have been acquired in any other way. Not the fragile confidence of someone who has never been seriously tested, but the durable, earned strength of someone who was tested, faltered, and learned to keep climbing. This is the person who is prepared more fully than before for the next mountain. Not because the next mountain will be easier, but because this climber is genuinely different from the one who began the first ascent.

The climb doesn't erase hardship but shapes you into someone who can approach future challenges with more wisdom, resilience, and joy after overcoming tough trials.

You have come a long way. Not just in the reading of this book, but in the living of the journey it describes. The PIT, the darkness, forced changes, and the interior work of transformation were not detours from the life you were meant to live. They form the foundation of the person who is now ready to live differently.

The mountain is ahead. Its terrain will test what has been built in you. Its summit will reveal what the valley could not show. The perspective you gain at the summit, achieved through your hard work, maintained by faith in yourself, and shaped by your unique blend of challenges and blessings, will make every part of the journey worthwhile.

You are more ready than you know.

The mountain is the next step
and you are being prepared to climb it.

Chapter Fourteen

Beyond Knowing

Experiencing Intimacy with God

The Necessity of Knowing God

There is a difference between knowing about God and knowing God. The difference between the accumulated knowledge of theology and the lived experience of Divine intimacy. The first can be gained through study. The second requires something more costly: a willingness to be fully known and, in turn, transformed.

Most of us spend a considerable amount of time and energy managing the distance between ourselves and God just close enough to feel the connection, but far enough to retain control. We participate in spiritual practices without surrendering our spiritual sovereignty.

We often find ourselves acknowledging the presence of the Divine while simultaneously holding on to the carefully constructed lives we have built for ourselves. This acknowledgment stops the difficult work of reordering our lives that intimacy requires. This reflects a human tendency to receive the benefits of a relationship with our creator while avoiding the vulnerabilities.

Instead of surrendering control, we seek to maintain a safe distance, allowing us to feel connected to the Divine without risking the discomfort of truly being open and exposed. This instinct is not evidence of insincerity but of our natural inclination to protect ourselves from the change that intimacy necessitates. It is a way of balancing our longing for connection with our fear of truly letting go.

This chapter is about what becomes possible when that barrier finally gives way. When the structure gives way by collapsing not through willpower but through exhaustion. It is about the restoration that precedes intimacy, wisdom and understanding that deepens, and the oneness that is available to anyone who has decided to stop justifying and simply surrender.

Laying the Foundation of Restoration

Intimacy is impossible without first acknowledging and addressing the underlying brokenness within ourselves and our relationships. Before a deeper connection can be established, it is imperative to confront the damage that has occurred, assess it honestly, and begin the necessary repair work. This reality is unpopular and uncomfortable; there is a natural tendency to want to move forward, focusing solely on what is possible, rather than pausing to examine what has been wounded or fractured.

However, intimacy cannot be built upon wounds that remain unaddressed and hidden. Attempting to construct closeness without bringing these issues into the light only results in a fragile foundation, one that is incapable of sustaining a true connection. The process requires a commitment to illuminate the broken places, to face them openly, and to allow healing to occur before moving forward.

This honest engagement with brokenness is the necessary groundwork for building authentic intimacy. It is only when the wounds are acknowledged and tended to that the possibility for real connection emerges. In this way, the journey toward intimacy begins not with avoidance or denial, but with courage and the willingness to bring what is broken into the light and to engage in the work of restoration.

Restoration begins with acknowledgment: the honest recognition of the distance that has grown, the ways in which the relationship with the Divine has been neglected or avoided, the specific wounds, resentments and failures that have accumulated as barriers. This acknowledgment is not self-condemnation. It is the prerequisite for everything that follows.

Forgiveness is essential to the spiritual journey, both in giving and receiving. We are invited to forgive those who have wounded us, even when the harm is real, and to accept forgiveness for our own failures and shortcomings. Unforgiveness toward others creates an inner hardness that closes us off to spiritual transformation. Likewise, refusing forgiveness for ourselves keeps us distant from the grace that is our birthright and inheritance.

What is most important to understand about restoration is that it is not primarily our work. God can restore what is broken, regardless of whether we deserve it. The Divine movement toward us in restoration is not a response to our sufficient preparation. It is grace, extended before we were ready to receive it, waiting only for our willingness to accept it.

Cultivating Wisdom and Understanding

Even if the foundation of restoration is imperfect, the process will gradually lead inward toward wisdom, understanding, and knowledge that can't be gained externally or hurried.

Wisdom, in the spiritual sense, is not the accumulation of correct information. It is something more fundamental: the capacity for discernment, which is the ability to perceive what is true, good, and aligned with Divine purpose. It is the difference between knowing the principles and knowing how that principle applies.

This wisdom sought through prayer not based on obligation but through an intimate inquiry. Through the study of sacred texts from multiple traditions, each of which carries partial light on the nature of the Divine. Through the counsel of spiritually mature people who have walked further along the path and who have earned the right to speak into the lives of those who are climbing. And through the slow, often uncomfortable practice of living according to what is understood, tested and refined in ways that study alone can never produce.

At the core of every religious tradition lies a source that surpasses the boundaries of any single tradition's explanation or narrative. This recognition invites a posture of openness, curiosity and a willingness to acknowledge that no one tradition possesses the entirety of truth about the Divine. Such humility in seeking is itself an act of reverence, honoring both the mystery of God and the sincere efforts of those who have gone before us.

Across the span of history, billions of people have reached out toward the Divine in diverse ways, shaped by their cultures, languages, and unique spiritual journeys. Each faith tradition reflects an authentic attempt to encounter and articulate the sacred, offering different perspectives that, together, enrich the tapestry of spiritual understanding.

When we invest time and effort to learn about other faiths, we gain a perspective that can illuminate and deepen our own understanding of God. The willingness to listen and learn from differing paths allows us to perceive new facets of the Divine, expanding our awareness and appreciation of the universality that lies at the heart of all authentic spiritual seeking.

Gaining Understanding

Complementary to wisdom is understanding, which represents the inner capacity to grasp what is true not simply on an intellectual level, but in a manner that resonates deeply with our soul. This form of understanding transcends the acquisition of knowledge, moving into a space where truth is felt and lived. It is not just about knowing facts or principles; it is about internalizing them in such a way that shape perspectives, actions, and relationships.

This understanding allows a person to connect with the Divine and with others by inhabiting truth. It bridges the gap between theory and practice with compassionate engagement and spiritual realities. Through this empathic insight, wisdom is enriched and grounded, becoming something that can be embodied and expressed in daily living.

Where wisdom discerns the right path, understanding feels its texture. Where wisdom provides the framework, understanding supplies compassion and empathy.

Spiritual understanding means having a unique ability to sense how God views the human experience. The Divine is not only found in the abstract of a distant God who simply knows all things. Moreover, in the closeness of a presence that feels your suffering and witnesses your journey intimately.

The descent into the PIT, those dark and difficult moments were not outside the scope of the sacred narrative. Instead, it was written into the story with intention, chosen and shaped specifically for you. It is only upon emerging from that depth, looking back with perspective, that the true purpose and meaning comes into view. The journey was not solitary; it was accompanied, and the significance of each step becomes clearer only in hindsight, as you recognize the path you have traversed.

This kind of understanding grows through quiet reflection and the willingness to be still long enough for something deeper than ordinary thought to gently rise within you. Through reflective journaling that processes experience against spiritual truth. Through the gradual, patient integration of what has been learned in the difficult seasons into a more coherent and compassionate understanding of both the self and the Divine.

The understanding of the cyclical nature of life with the rhythm of beginnings, middles, and endings is woven into every relationship, every period of growth, and every chapter of this book. This ongoing pattern is more than just a simple repetition; it serves as a form of Divine instruction, offering guidance and meaning within the spiritual journey.

Each cycle, whether it marks the start of something new, the steady progression through challenges, or the conclusion of a season, carries its own lessons. The transitions between these phases invite reflection and openness to change, encouraging an awareness of how endings create the foundation for new beginnings. By attuning ourselves to this rhythm, we learn to recognize our place within it and trust that each stage is purposeful, leading us toward deeper spiritual understanding.

Learning to read this rhythm and recognize where you are within it create the conditions for new beginnings is one of the greatest principles of spiritual understanding.

The Fruits of Intimacy

As restoration is laid as wisdom and understanding is cultivated, something begins to emerge which is different from anything an intellectual or religious life alone can produce - knowledge of God. Knowledge of God in the intimacy of actual encounter, lived in the body, felt in the spirit, expressed in the specific texture of a daily life that has been reorganized around a relationship rather than around a set of beliefs.

The growth of this intimacy is often impeded by attachments that operate beneath the level of conscious awareness: codependences and "soul ties" bonds formed through past wounds or unmet needs that divert emotional and spiritual energy away from the Divine and toward the people or circumstances on which we have become unhealthily dependent.

These attachments are not malevolent in their origin. They are formed responses to real needs in specific moments of vulnerability. They have calcified into patterns that now constrain rather than protect keeping us bound to sources of comfort or validation that were never equipped to provide what only the Divine can give. The wisdom, understanding, and knowledge cultivated in the journey inward serve as the tools for identifying these patterns honestly and for beginning the work of redirecting our dependencies toward self and God.

Freedom from these attachments is not the cold independence of a person who needs no one. It is the warm, grounded freedom of a person whose fundamental security is rooted in something that cannot be taken away and who can give out of abundance rather than from the anxious need to receive something in return.

Trusting the Inner Voice

In navigating a spiritual life particularly in the discernment of what is genuine versus what is distraction, what is Divine direction versus what is merely the noise becomes an essential guide.

The quiet inner knowing is developed and refined through the entire journey of this book, is reliable when properly practiced. This inner knowing is nurtured by spiritual discipline which grows being shaped by experiences, reflection, and the willingness to sit in stillness. Over time, it becomes a trustworthy guide in navigating the complexities of spiritual life, allowing discernment between Divine direction and the distractions of desire or fear. This process is not a single event, but an ongoing commitment to authenticity, patience, and openness, ensuring that the guidance received remains grounded and true.

Distractions are the primary threat to spiritual clarity. The temporal allurements that consume our attention fragment our focus not all of which are harmful in themselves but compete with the quality of attention that Divine intimacy requires. Recognizing these distractions for what they are and choosing to redirect our attention toward what is essential is one of the most practical forms of spiritual discipline.

The saying "hurt people hurt people" applies here in a profound and specific way. Unhealed wounds rarely remain confined to the person who carries them. They spill into our relationships, shape our spiritual lives, and affect every attempt at genuine connection. This is why the healing work woven throughout this book is not an exercise in self-indulgence; it is essential. Healing creates the space for deeper intimacy with God and for the authentic human relationships that spiritual wholeness makes possible.

Experiencing Oneness

The journey toward intimacy with God is something that those who have encountered it recognize it immediately. This is not the erasure of self into some indistinct nor the loss of individuality. Rather, it is the profound harmony of a spirit brought fully into alignment with a deep and intimate union with the Divine. Individuality is not destroyed but fulfilled in the highest expression of the human experience.

The comfort found here is not derived from a life free of challenges; instead, it is anchored in a peace that remains steadfast even during adversity. This peace, unshaken by hardship, is the sign of a spirit that has found its place in connection with the Divine.

This oneness is characterized by alignment: the coherence of desires and divine will moving in the same direction. The peace that comes not from having resolved every question but from having stopped fighting the one who holds the answers. The clarity of a life becomes simplified not because the complexity has disappeared, but because the complexity which is organized becomes clear and trustworthy.

Once you know, you know. The experience of oneness carries its own authority. It needs no witness, confirmation, or second opinion from the world. It arrives as peace not the peace of resignation, but the deep stillness that follows a long and exhausting war finally brought to an end. It settles into the heart in the moment displacing the machinery of the self-made life, and the soul no longer struggling to carry what it was never meant to bear alone. Peace arrives with the realization: this is what I sought all along. Every chapter, misstep, and unnamed longing led me here.

God and Me

I want to tell you about a prayer I said at the age of twenty-one years old that took me nearly decade to understand.

I was sitting in my car outside a Circle K convenience store, waiting for my girlfriend to come back. While she was inside, I prayed not with surrender, because I was nowhere near that. I prayed with the careful, honest deliberate way, feeling the weight of God's attention pressing on me, but still was not ready to faithfully follow the Christian path.

I said, "God, I won't go far. I promise."

I knew God heard me because I knew. I was not ready to release control of my life based on my limited understanding. I knew exactly what I was doing: I was bargaining. I built boundaries around my life, keeping God near but not close enough to require real change. It was, I can see now with the clarity that only the passage of years provides, a profound act of being in control and choosing my girlfriend over God. It wasn't just about her it was my decision to keep God at a distance. It was me wanting to live my life the way I intended. I didn't want to be known as a "Holy Roller."

For the next couple of years, life appeared to be working. I transitioned from active duty into a federal job as an aircraft structural repair specialist purchasing my first home at the age of twenty-three. I had a girlfriend who was beautiful and who loved me in ways I was not yet equipped to fully receive. Externally, everything moved according to my self-made plan.

There were cracks, but I didn't know how to examine them. My girlfriend would sometimes weep tormented by past trauma, and I was utterly unable to reach her. I did not possess empathy or understanding that could comfort her. I called it overconfidence. Looking back, I see it more accurately as a limitation of not being broken enough to know his own depths.

For the next seven years, I made no serious effort to connect with God. My worldview grew quietly disenchanting, as worldviews built on self-sufficiency always eventually do. I had convinced myself that living without visible consequence for turning away was evidence that turning away was acceptable. It was a flawed test I was running on the universe patient as it is, was letting me run it.

When she finally left me, my heartbreak was devastating. I came to understand much later, it was precisely what I needed. Not because I deserved the pain, but because the pain was the specific instrument that broke something sealed shut for years. I needed to be alone. I needed to mature. I needed to stop managing the distance between myself and God and finally close it.

I fell to my knees not metaphorically, but literally, in the specific posture of a person who has run out of other options. I prayed with simplicity and honesty that I had not since childhood. This wasn't my first prayer but a second after many years. The first prayer was months earlier while away at Chanute AFB Base for some advance training in aircraft production control was the same place where it had begun seven years earlier after basic training. This time I asked God for three specific things: to get fit and lose weight; to be selected as an honor graduate; and to know whether the woman in my life at that time was meant to be my wife. Jokingly, I asked God to just give me two out of the three.

They were concrete requests almost transactional. Upon graduating with honors, and improving my fitness, she said, "no" and declined my invitation for marriage. Instead, she told me she was leaving.   That was the beginning of my PIT experience, season where my connection with God I had been avoiding was finally, fully made coming full circle. I can clearly see my arrogance now and how God honored my prayer request.

I have come to understand that prayer in that parking lot differently than I understood it then. It was not merely immaturity, though it was that. It was also, in its own strange way, a relationship with an acknowledgment that the presence was real, made by someone not yet ready to fully receive it. God did not abandon me in those seven years of distance. God waited. With the patience of something that is not threatened by our delays and does not stop being present simply because we have stopped paying attention.

The wound I carried through the PIT was deeper than any specific loss. It was the reflection of what I had done in that car: declared I would not go far and then go as far as I could. The pain of the PIT was, in part, the pain of a relationship that I had been keeping at arm's length while slowly starving for its fullness.

Oneness with God is profoundly real. I know this not as a theological position but as an experience with a specific weight and a specific history. We cannot experience its fullness until we are willing to stop negotiating the terms of our own surrender. The Divine helps us in our times of need not by making the path easy, but by drawing us closer to the flame of purification stripping away anything blocking the connection we most deeply need. This illustrates the conflict between our decisions and our spiritual goals.

What I discovered, on the far side of the PIT and the seven years of reconnection, was not a God who had been waiting to punish me for the bargain. It was God who had been waiting, simply and patiently, for me to be ready to stop bargaining. The peace that arrived when I finally stopped was not earned. It was given freely, immediately, and with a completeness that made the years of managing the distance feel, in retrospect, like an extraordinary waste of a gift that had been available all along.

Once you know, you know. There is a deep sense of peace that settles in the soul when a person finally allows the will of the Creator to take the place of their approach to life. This peace is not simply the absence of conflict or the quiet that follows surrender; it is a profound, interior calm that marks the end of striving against the One who knows best.

It is the moment when our self-sufficiency has insisted on its own way, is gently set aside and replaced by trust in something greater. In that space, the restless energy of self-direction gives way to a deep assurance, rooted in the knowledge that the Creator's will is both trustworthy and good. It is in this exchange that relinquishing our self-sufficiency for Divine guidance is where lasting peace is found allowing our soul to rest. Peace is the beginning of everything this book has been pointing toward.

Once You Know You Know

Chapter Fifteen

The Illuminated Path

Embracing Supernatural Guidance

The Dream

I want to start with a dream. I was nineteen years old, recently graduated from high school and freshly accepted to Northern Illinois University on academic probation, totally unprepared for the world ahead of me. I was academically challenged only reading a book once for pleasure. My mind was shaped by the South Side of Chicago - a place where institutions were dissolving; gang violence filled the streets, drug addiction and liquor stores outnumbering the places of worship and gas stations combined. Which caused the very fabric holding families together to begin fraying at the seams. I not only felt out of place in my neighborhood but also believed that I wasn't college material.

As I considered what college might look like for me, my imagination was filled with images of weekend parties, chasing girls, and smoking marijuana. Deep down, I recognized that my mindset was precisely the problem. I already knew exactly where that path would end, and I wanted more out of life than the routine of parties and a degree I might not earn.

During high school, I spent a lot of time hanging out downtown Chicago, frequenting places like the Warehouse, Mars Bar, Medusa's, and Mendel

Catholic High School, all drawn by my love for house music. When the East and West coasts were battling it out for rap music dominance, we were enjoying party music from radio stations like WGCI and WBMX feeding the multicultural house-head party scene. I partied my way through those years, attending a social gathering nearly every weekend. There truly was no place like Chicago, and the city's vibrant energy pulled me out of my mundane routine in Harvey, opening my eyes to new experiences, perspectives and people.

Looking back, I realized that while I had a lot of fun during high school, hanging out and going to parties became normal. By the time I was preparing for college, I was ready for a change but didn't know how to change any aspect of my life. The excitement of the streets and nightlife had shown me a world beyond Harvey, but it also left me yearning for something deeper and more meaningful.

The night before my departure to Northern Illinois University, I was weighed down by a heavy sense of uncertainty and offered a single, heartfelt prayer: *God, please give me direction.* That very night, my request was answered through a dream composed of four distinct visions that felt different and far more purposeful than any ordinary dream. At nineteen, these visions were entirely detached from my reality, yet they carried a sense of certainty that I could not ignore.

The dream revealed four specific visions of something I hadn't yet imagined: a dark cloud descending over my hometown of Harvey, a woman named Darla, a vision of myself in military, and fireworks over the Golden Gate Bridge.

Reflecting on that night, I realize how impossible those predictions seemed at the time, as I had no plans for the military, no knowledge of the location of the Gold Gate Bridge, the darkness that would befall my beloved hometown, and never hearing the name Darla ever spoken . Yet, the dream served as a definitive turning point, replacing my confusion with a mysterious but resolute sense of guidance. The visions ultimately provided the compass I had prayed for, quietly shaping the course of my life in the years that followed.

There was no dramatic narrative, no voice echoing from above, no angelic figure breaking through the night. Instead, the dream was clear, vivid, and unmistakably steady. This dream didn't fade away like most dreams do after waking. This one held its shape carrying a quiet but undeniable sense of assurance. This feeling marked something far more meaningful than a typical dream.

The dream had a sense of significance that went far beyond the fleeting images or random thoughts. It was different and something I could not easily dismiss. Unlike memories that reference the past, this dream offered no connection to my earlier experiences. Instead, it pointed toward a future I had neither encountered nor even imagined totally unfamiliar to me.

In that moment, I recognized the dream was more than just a dream but spiritual direction. It was not just a collection of disconnected scenes, but a purposeful message guiding me toward an unknown future, marking the beginning of a journey shaped by something greater than myself.

The next morning, I told my parents I would not be attending college, and I would be joining the Marines. My mother started to cry and my father remained quiet. I understood, yet I still went. I headed to the recruiter's office in Harvey; when I arrived, the Marine and Navy recruiters were out for lunch. The only person there was Staff Sergeant Green, an Air Force recruiter, who sat at his desk as if he had been waiting for me. I told him I was ready to join the military and that I wanted to leave as soon as possible. He scheduled me for the ASVAB, shook my hand, and that was it.

Three months later, I set out for basic training at Lackland Air Force Base in San Antonio Texas. Everything I owned fit into a few bags, but what weighed most was the dream I kept quietly to myself and a steady assurance that I was finally moving in the right direction. For the first time in my life, I felt a sense of certainty and purpose guiding me. It was not confidence born from achievement or certainty about what lay ahead, but rather the settled knowledge that I was following a path illuminated by something beyond my own understanding. Carrying this dream with me, I embarked on a journey that would shape the course of my life, trusting that the direction I'd received was leading me exactly where I needed to go.

Following basic training, I was sent to technical school at Chanute Air Force Base in Illinois for three months of specialized training in aircraft structural repair. There, we mastered the art of restoring battle-damaged aircraft, learning exactly what it took to get a plane back into the fight. It was there when I received orders to be stationed at Lakenheath Air Force Base in the United Kingdom but a fellow classmate offered to swap his California orders for mine because he was from the state and wanted to see the world. I accepted knowing that this was an opportunity which aligned with my dream setting my path in motion. McClellan Air Force Base in Sacramento, California became my first duty station.

Three of us had the same follow-on assignment, so we decided to drive across the country together. During the drive my friend Ed, who is a Born-Again Christian, invited me to visit a few local churches. He was the first person I felt comfortable enough to share the details of my dream that was shaping my sense of direction. He said that God was tugging at my heart, and this guidance wasn't a coincidence, but Divinely inspired.

I took us five days to drive across country. We arrived on a Thursday and that following Sunday morning we set off to grab some chow before going to church. We left the base driving in one direction, stopping at the first church we saw, which was First Evangelistic Free Church.

We arrived early, finding the parking lot completely empty. With no one else around, we remained by the car, quietly waiting. A few moments later, the church doors opened and a young woman stepped outside. She walked across the parking lot toward us with a welcoming smile. As she approached, she extended a warm greeting.

"Hi, my name is Darla. Welcome to our church. What are your names?"

Ed and I immediately exchanged a glance, silently acknowledging the significance of her name: Darla had appeared in my dream, and now here she was before us. Ed pointed to the sky, a gesture that underscored the uncanny connection between the dream and this moment.

Despite the recognition, I felt uneasy and overwhelmed by the reality of experiencing something I had only seen in a dream. The encounter was unsettling, and I found myself wanting to leave, but I stayed until service ended. That day marked both my first and last visit to the church, and it was the only time I would ever see Darla.

A few years later, I stood with someone I loved dearly watching the 4th of July fireworks exploding over the Golden Gate Bridge reminding me of my dream. In that moment, I realized that I was truly living out the path revealed in my dream. Every step I took felt intentional, as if I was moving forward according to a purpose greater than my own. It felt as though the dream itself was traveling with me, providing both direction and companionship as I navigated the uncertainties of life.

This is what it means to walk an illuminated path. Not the romantic notion of a life without difficulty or uncertainty, but the specific, lived experience of receiving direction that transcends your own understanding and then discovering, in the fullness of time, that the direction was trustworthy. The dream was more than a premonition.

It was a spiritual encounter opening a door through which my entire life would eventually pass. It became my undeniable evidence that the Divine was not only real but personal and engaging in the unfolding of my particular life.

Recognizing the Need for Guidance

To understand why that dream arrived when it did, you need to understand where I was standing when I received it. I had grown up spiritually minded in a way that was never fully connected to the life around me. I had known, from an early age, that God was real not as a theological conclusion but as a felt certainty, the same kind of knowing I had at six years old asking who God was and feeling, for the first time, genuinely alive. But knowing God was real and living in alignment with that reality were two entirely different things.

We were poor not only financially, though that was true, but poor in the deeper sense of a worldview that had not yet been expanded. In high school, I compared my life to my peers and always felt uneasy with my reality.

I believed we lived in the ugliest house in the neighborhood. Our house was like living on a construction site. My father would start a project and wouldn't finish it before he started another project. He had a successful painting business, stayed busy renovating other people's homes never finishing his own.

I witnessed how many young people in my community had not cultivated visions for anything different. The poverty mindset I observed around me was contagious with many having a limited imagination to challenge the way things had always been. We were all poor, but I was truly uncomfortable with this fact.

Today the neighborhood is still suffering from the remnants of the economic impact of thousands of factory job losses and White flight of the 1970s, giving Black homeowners the opportunity to purchase homes in a declining real estate market where grocery stores and other businesses closed their doors. The only thing which remained was Saint Susanna Catholic Church which eventually ended its worship services.

Mayor Daley's city revitalization effort compounded the decline by relocating thousands of poor, predominantly Black families from high-density Chicago projects to the south suburbs, transforming our community almost overnight. Local politicians were inept to repel the gang violence which arrived or stop the decline of local businesses. Even the new Dixie Square Mall closed its doors. They used the mall as a movie set for the Blues Brothers movie. The mall stayed abandoned for decades, bearing the skid marks from stunt drivers who left their rubble behind as a community reminder.

If you drive through Harvey today, you'll find more abandoned houses than non-abandoned. Each street reveals an overgrown glimpse into the past where gaps of knowledge seem to be no longer relevant. Future generations in this community are ill equipped to build sustainable ecosystems which would benefit their families and society at large. The moral and social infrastructure that once held this neighborhood together quietly dissolved.

The dark cloud I had seen in a teenager's dream was the shadow of what was coming. The environment had instilled certain limitations, making it even more difficult to envision a path forward to a better life. Surrounded by a community grappling with its own struggles, it became clear that I needed something beyond myself to navigate the uncertainty to move beyond the constraints of my circumstances.

The direction I required was not something I could manufacture; it had to come from a source greater than my own understanding. And the dream arrived precisely at the intersection of need and openness, in the moment just before I would have made the choice that shaped everything.

Divine guidance tends to arrive when we have become genuinely ready to ask the questions: Who am I? Why was I created? Who is God?

Embracing Supernatural Guidance

The illuminated path begins with the willingness to receive guidance that originates beyond our own reasoning and to act on it before we have confirmation. This is not the comfortable faith of looking back at a provision already received, but the demanding faith of moving forward based on direction.

This kind of guidance comes in many forms. Dreams and visions, as in my own experience, are among the most ancient and cross-culturally consistent forms of Divine communication recorded across many of the world's spiritual traditions. It also arrives through the quiet inner knowing that surfaces in prayer and meditation.

The clarity that rises above competing desires and fears reveals a path that feels deeply and authentically true. Through the convergence of circumstances that seem too specific to be accidental. Through the counsel of people whose words arrive at precisely the moment are needed and carries the weight the moment requires.

The dream I received was not a product of my conscious desires. I had no particular orientation toward military service before it arrived. It came from somewhere other than my own planning, and it pointed toward a life I could not have designed for myself. It took me a long time to commit to this way of living by faith, but I am glad I finally did.

Supernatural guidance is not achieved through striving, merit, or the attempt to earn grace. The work lies in preparing the inner landscape by creating conditions within oneself that allow for the extraordinary to be received and recognized. This preparation is not about deserving; it is about making space. By intentionally quieting the distractions and busyness of ordinary life, one becomes more able to notice and respond to signals that originate beyond everyday experience. The process involves fostering an interior stillness that makes it possible to discern spiritual guidance that transcends one's own understanding.

Fasting, prayer, and meditation are common in many traditions because they quiet the ego and create inner stillness for deeper awareness. The mind that is perpetually occupied with distraction, entertainment, and the management of surface concerns is not incapable of receiving Divine guidance. It is simply too loud to hear it.

The Inner Confidence of Alignment

Receiving and acting on Divine guidance demonstrates an inner confidence that has nothing to do with arrogance or certainty about outcomes. It is the confidence of alignment: the settled sense of moving in a direction that is right, even when the terrain is difficult, and the destination is not yet visible.

This confidence does not eliminate fear. The morning after my dream, when I told my parents I was not going to college and was joining the military instead, I was not without apprehension. I was stepping into something I could not fully see, based on images from a dream. But beneath the apprehension was something steadier: the quiet, unshakeable conviction that this was the direction. That conviction which I have come to understand as the felt signature of Divine guidance is itself a form of strength, available to anyone who has cultivated the interior life necessary to recognize it.

Navigating with Intention and Resolve

Receiving supernatural guidance is the beginning, not the end, of the illuminated path. What follows the reception is the sustained, daily work of navigating in alignment with what was received through the tests, distractions and stretches of difficulty that any significant path inevitably includes.

Difficulties encountered along the guided path do not indicate that the guidance itself is flawed or that we have deviated from it. Rather, these challenges serve as mechanisms by which guidance is integrated into practice, transforming theoretical knowledge into actionable wisdom.

Each test navigated with faith not the naive faith that expects difficulty to vanish, but the mature faith that moves through hardship with trust intact deepens both the capacity for discernment and the relationship with the Divine from which that guidance flows. This is how illumination accumulates: not through a single dramatic encounter, but through the sustained practice of choosing alignment over the pull of distraction, day after day, test after test, until the orientation becomes the default rather than the deliberate choice.

The commitment required for the illuminated path is not occasional. It is daily. The distractions that compete for attention are not always harmful in themselves can be simply the ordinary demands of a full human life. They all compete with the quality of focused, sustained attention that spiritual development requires.

Recognizing what is essential and protecting it is a discipline that must be woven into the fabric of daily life. This process begins by establishing consistent practices that reinforce the commitment to the illuminated path. These practices serve as anchors, ensuring that the core values and guidance received remain central amidst the inevitable distractions and demands of everyday living.

The conscious curation of what is allowed to occupy interior life is fundamental. It requires intentional decisions about which thoughts, influences, and activities are permitted to shape one's inner world. By being selective about what enters the mind and heart, one creates an environment where clarity and purpose can thrive, free from the noise that might otherwise obscure direction.

Surrounding oneself with people who support rather than undermine the received direction strengthens resolve and provides encouragement. These supportive connections help maintain focus, offering both accountability and affirmation in moments of challenge or doubt.

The practical work of staying the course lies in the commitment to these structures and relationships. By continuously affirming what is essential and guarding it through daily practice, one cultivates the resilience and stability needed to navigate the illuminated path. This ongoing stewardship ensures that the guidance received is not lost but remains an active force shaping every step forward.

It is not glamorous. It is also not optional. The illuminated path does not maintain itself. It requires the ongoing stewardship of the person walking it.

The framework of PIT and TIP (Place in Time and Time in Place) remains relevant here. Each stage of the journey serves a distinct purpose, and the ability to identify your current phase and understand its specific demands is an important aspect of insight. Certain seasons call for active engagement; others call for patient waiting. Certain periods are crucibles; others are harvests. Learning to read the season accurately, and to respond to it appropriately rather than imposing the wrong response at the right moment, is the ongoing work of the illuminated life.

Reaching New Horizons

The person who has committed to the illuminated path has cultivated the receptivity to receive guidance, the faith to act on it before it is verified, and the resolve to navigate the tests with trust intact. A quality of life that could not have been reached by any other route.

It is not a life defined by the absence of difficulty, nor by the guarantee that every outcome will arrive exactly as imagined. It is a life guided by direction and stability, where every action reflects alignment to purpose.

The spiritual fullness that emerges from a life walked in alignment with Divine guidance is not the fullness of having achieved everything desired. It is the fullness of having become someone through the formation of the PIT, through the tests navigated, through the guidance received and acted upon, and whose inner life is genuinely coherent. Whose desires and values and actions are moving in the same direction.

This fullness generates clarity: the capacity to see with greater precision what matters and what does not, what is aligned with purpose or merely noise, and the next steps. Clarity of this kind is not the same as intellectual brilliance. It is the practical fruit of sustained spiritual attentiveness, which is available to anyone willing to cultivate it, regardless of formal education, natural intelligence, or worldly achievement.

The dream was the first great confirmation of my illuminated path. But it was not the last. The nature of Divine guidance is cumulative, with each confirmation deepens the trust that makes the next act of faith slightly less difficult and the next step slightly more assured.

Over a lifetime, these confirmations accumulate into something that I can only call peace, not the peace of a life that has been easy, but the peace of a life that has been accompanied. The knowledge, built from specific evidence gathered across specific experiences, that the guidance was real, that it was trustworthy, that the path it illuminated led somewhere worth going.

This peace dwells in me today. The dream illuminated my path toward spirituality and the lifelong journey unto wisdom and understanding. And every step since the PIT, the mountain, the desert of Kuwait, the man at the door who knew my grandparents' names, the woman on the shuttle bus, the moment on the waterbed, the prayers at Chanute Air Force Base, and the fireworks over the Golden Gate Bridge has been part of the same illuminated path that the dream first pointed toward.

Throughout this journey, I've come to realize that the guidance I sought was always present. It was not something I needed to search for or strive to create, but rather something that quietly accompanied me at every step, waiting for my recognition and trust. The path was illuminated not by dramatic revelations, but by a steady presence that called for my faith.

Learning to trust this guidance was an essential part of my development. It required me to let go of the need for certainty and embrace the conviction that the direction being revealed was both real and reliable. The guidance was a constant companion, offering reassurance even through uncertainty and challenge, so long as I was willing to listen and respond with faith.

By choosing to trust in the ever-present guidance, I found the support I needed to continue my journey. Each time I acted in alignment with this inner direction, my confidence in it grew, reinforcing the understanding that I was never alone and that the guidance was trustworthy. Every step forward became an affirmation that the path, though sometimes difficult, was illuminated by a wisdom greater than my own.

Divine wisdom does not shout over the noise;
it waits for the stillness.

Chapter Sixteen

The Gateway of Surrender

Accepting Life's Transitions

Releasing Control

The ultimate surrender is not the surrender of a battle. It is the surrender of the belief that the battle was ever ours to win by force.

We arrive at this chapter having traveled a long distance. Through the PIT and the ascent. Through the darkness of depression and the slow return of light. Through the desert solitude and the breakthrough and climbing the mountain. And somewhere in all of that traveling, most of us have discovered the same thing: that the tools we arrived with the willpower, strategies, and the relentless application of intelligence to the problems of human life are necessary but not sufficient. They carry us far but not all the way.

There is a place on the journey where we must open our hands. Where the grip that has been the source of so much stability must become the posture of offering rather than grasping. Where the trust that has been developing through the previous chapters must finally be extended to the one thing which is the outcome itself.

This chapter explores this sacred space. The gateway of surrender represents an important turning point along our journey, where we face the reality that pure determination and control have their limits. Crossing this threshold comes at a high cost: letting go of our plans and the belief that we can manage or predict life. Embracing surrender takes both bravery and openness by cultivating the willingness to let go of certainty, opening ourselves up to possibilities beyond our understanding.

On the other side of this gateway, something new and profound becomes available. Relief and freedom are not found through striving, tighter control, or relentless effort. It emerges when we surrender. What could not be attained through force becomes accessible when our soul finally releases its grip and entrusts itself to Divine understanding.

Stepping through the gateway of surrender marks a shift in the journey from holding tightly toward a controlled release. This relief is not merely the absence of difficulty, but a sense of liberation from the burdens that once weighed heavily. It signals the arrival of a freedom that was previously out of reach, a freedom born of letting go and entrusting the outcome to the Divine.

The act of surrender opens the door to new possibilities and allows for the emergence of peace, clarity, and acceptance. This transformation is not instant, but grows as one continues to trust and embrace the guidance that accompanies the journey. The gateway of surrender marks a crucial turning point, opening the door to greater peace and a renewed approach to life defined by relief, freedom, and faith.

It is not simply the absence of difficulty, but the presence of a deeper peace rooted in trust, acceptance, and the realization that guidance and support are always present. This transformation brings clarity and coherence to one's inner life, aligning desires, values, and actions in a way that was never possible while holding control. The gateway of surrender marks a passage into a life shaped by faith, trust, and spiritual fullness.

The Threshold of Choice

Every profound transition in life invites a reexamination of the tools that have carried us this far. We arrive at these thresholds equipped with strategies forged through experience, carrying the hard-earned skills of those who have survived previous storms through determination, intelligence, and strength of will. These tools are not failures. They are the very instruments which enabled us to endure, overcome, and advance. The problem is the belief that they are sufficient. That if we think hard enough, plan carefully, work diligently, and maintain control tightly enough, we can navigate every terrain that life presents.

While the belief in our ability to manage life's challenges serves us well during everyday struggles, it reaches its limits in the face of adversities that are simply beyond our control. These moments expose the inadequacy of determination, planning, and productivity revealing circumstances where no amount of effort can change the outcome. Sudden losses, illnesses that resist even the strongest resolve, and griefs that persist regardless of how industrious we are all demonstrate the comprehensive failure of this belief. In these situations, the tools that once brought us stability and progress prove insufficient, compelling us to confront the reality that some forces cannot be managed or overcome through sheer will alone.

It is at these encounters that the threshold of surrender appears. Not as a comfortable invitation but as a confrontation: the undeniable recognition that what we have been relying on is not enough, and that something different is required. Something that looks, from the outside and from within the framework of self-sufficiency, uncomfortably like giving up.

It is not giving up. It is the most courageous act available at the threshold, which is the decision to release the illusion of absolute control and to trust in something larger than the self. To unclench the fists that have been gripping the reins of life and to open the hands as a compassionate offering. This is surrender not passive or defeated, but active, deliberate and deeply faithful.

Before we can surrender what, we have been carrying, we need to understand why. This requires the kind of honest self-examination that runs throughout this book: the courageous observation of our natural default settings encompassing our emotional responses, coping strategies, and the specific forms we use to control the illusion when it is threatened.

Some of us control our lives through planning, building elaborate structures of contingency against every possible difficulty. And some through relationship management, carefully orchestrating the people around us to minimize the risk of being hurt or disappointed. While others control through productivity, staying so busy that deeper fears never have enough quietness to surface. Each of these patterns has its logic. Each in its own way.

A quiet shift in the recognition that one season is ending, old ways no longer work, and a new orientation is needed. To prepare for this change is to honor that inner knowing, reflecting on what has been learned in the previous chapters, releasing rigid expectations, and cultivating readiness to walk on an unfamiliar path.

The Lessons of Letting Go

There are few sorrows worse than losing a parent. Losing both parents changed how I saw myself and my standing in this world. Both of my parents had been part of my life from the very beginning of my existence and now they are gone.

The experience of losing both parents has profoundly shifted my perspective on the nature of existence. Their passing has deepened my understanding of how temporal life really is. Their presence had always anchored my sense of self and belonging in the world. Now in their absence, I am confronted with the undeniable truth that all relationships and moments in all forms are fleeting.

This realization does not diminish the significance of what was shared but instead brings clarity to the preciousness of every connection and the importance of embracing the present. In recognizing the impermanence of life, I am reminded to cherish those I love and to appreciate each day, knowing that nothing is guaranteed and everything is subject to change.

As a child, the fear of losing my mother was a constant presence in my life. This fear was not some vague or distant anxiety; it was real and immediate, shaped by what I witnessed in middle school. I saw first-hand how my friend Ricky struggled under the weight of grief after his mother died of cancer. Her passing was more than he could process, and the pain of her absence overwhelmed him, sending him into a deep depression that altered his personality which he carried into high school.

Seeing Ricky's devastation left a lasting impression on me. His experience became a living illustration of what it means to lose someone you love and depend on for everything. It was as if his grief revealed my own worst fears of losing your lifeline. The vulnerability of childhood dependence on those closest to us meant that the possibility of loss was not just theoretical, but an ever-present shadow, shaping how I understood love, attachment, and the fragility of life itself.

When my parents died each loss carried its own particular weight. The preparation I thought I had made was both more and less than I needed. More in the sense that the spiritual work of the preceding years had given me something to stand on. Less, in the sense that no preparation fully insulates you from the specific gravity of losing someone whose existence has been part of your architecture.

What I am still learning is that the deepest lessons never fully arrive but keep unfolding when you lose someone: learning to hold on and let go. Holding on feels like loyalty. It feels like grief is honoring the person but unable to move forward as a refusal to forget. What it produces, over time, is a life organized around an absence shaped by what is no longer there rather than by what remains and what is still possible.

Letting go is not forgetting. It is not the erasure of love or the minimization of loss. It is the conscious decision to allow the grief to move through you to feel its full weight without letting that weight become the permanent structure of your existence. When I finally let go, the relief was profound and specific: not the relief of having solved a problem, but the relief of having put down something that was never meant to be carried indefinitely.

Annie's Story

I want to tell you about a woman I'll call Annie, whose story has stayed with me because it represents a quality of surrender that I have encountered almost nowhere else.

Annie lost her son. He was not a gang member, not someone whose death could be filed under the predictable tragedies of a dangerous life. He was an aspiring filmmaker a handsome young man full of potential, purpose, and goodness. He radiated the kind of God-given promise that makes its loss feel not just tragic, but cosmically wrong. She held on to her faith despite his body never being recovered.

She was left not only with the grief of losing her only son but with the unresolvable anguish of a loss that has no grave to visit, and no definitive ending to anchor her mourning. The absence of closure intensified her sorrow, making it impossible to find comfort in ritual or finality. Without a place to lay flowers or say goodbye, Annie's mourning remained suspended in uncertainty, amplifying the pain and complicating the process of healing.

This unique aspect of her loss meant that her grief was not only about missing her son, but also about living with questions that could never be answered and a heartache that could not be contained by the boundaries of traditional grief. She faithfully endured unimaginable hardship. It was not a faith sustained effortlessly, nor was it free from the profound emotional toll that accompanies deep grief. Her journey was marked by the struggle of wrestling with God which is a characteristic of authentic faith.

Importantly, Annie did not give in to despair. Her surrender was not a surrender to hopelessness; instead, it was a surrender to God. This distinction is crucial, though it often becomes blurred in the depths of irretrievable loss. The difference between surrendering to despair and surrendering to God, while subtle in moments of anguish, defines the courage and resilience that she demonstrated. Despite challenges and uncertainty, she relied on her foundation made of faith.

Annie's example was a masterclass in the specific kind of surrender this chapter is about. Not the surrender of someone whose losses were manageable. Not the faith of someone who was spared. The surrender of someone who was given the worst that life can offer, and who chose daily without the comfort of resolution but to trust in God who holds what she could not.

Watching Annie navigate that loss solidified something in me about the nature of acceptance. There are griefs that cannot be resolved. There are losses that will never make any sense in the way our minds demand them to make sense. The faith that navigates these losses is not the faith of explanation. It is the faith of presence and the willingness to keep showing up, to keep the conversation with God open, even when the conversation includes the rawest, most unguarded expressions of pain.

Surrendering at its deepest level is not the clean release of something you are ready to let go of, but the agonizing, faithful release of something you would give anything to keep.

Letting go is not learned in easy seasons.

Stepping Through the Gateway

The inner realignment that surrender produces is not a single event. It is a process of moving through the mind, body, and spirit in a sequence that cannot be forced or rushed, only accompanied.

The first movement of surrender is mental. Recognizing mental patterns such as negative self-talk, limiting beliefs, and the persistent inner critic is essential to overcoming resistance to surrendering. These patterns are not random. They are the mind's reasonable attempts to protect itself from further harm: if I don't hope, I won't be disappointed; if I don't trust, I won't be betrayed; if I maintain control, I won't have to face what happens when I lose control.

Understanding how our mind tries to protect us is essential to the work of surrender. This compassionate recognition does not condemn our patterns for existing. It sees them as strategies that were once necessary for survival but have gradually become more restrictive.

Transformation begins by honoring the protective function of those patterns while also telling the truth about their resistance. What once served as a shield may, over time, become a barrier. Only when we hold both realities together can we begin to loosen our grip on old defenses not with force or self-judgment, but gently, with awareness. And in that loosening, space opens for new patterns of trust, and openness where the process of surrendering can emerge.

What emerges on the other side of this recognition is not fearlessness but a different relationship with fear which is the capacity to feel it without being governed by it. To trust over apprehension, not because the apprehension has disappeared, but because something has been recognized as more trustworthy than the fear's worst projections. Faith means choosing to act, even when doubts remain.

Surrender is not only a mental event. It inhabits the body by loosening of the chronic tension that sustained vigilance produces, in the slower breath of a person who has stopped bracing for impact, in the quality of rest that becomes available when the exhausting work of managing everything finally stops.

Honoring the body as the vessel of spiritual experience means attending to it with the same intentionality brought to the interior life: adequate rest, nourishment, movement, the physical practices that create conditions in which sustained spiritual attentiveness is possible. The body is not incidental to the spiritual journey. It is its address.

Spiritually, the transition of surrender involves a quiet and deliberate turning away from the noise of the world long enough to hear Divine guidance. This is the quieting of our attention: the active, receptive stillness of a person who has decided to listen more than to speak, to receive more than to manage, to trust more than to control.

Rather than focusing on controlling or orchestrating every outcome, this practice invites us to become open and attentive. It is about stepping back from the urge to manage, allowing ourselves to be shaped by what comes instead of forcing what we think should arrive.

At the heart of this quieting is trust. The willingness to let go of the need for control and to surrender to a larger wisdom creates space for inner peace. By choosing trust, we foster an environment where guidance, clarity, and comfort can emerge naturally, without the strain of constant management.

Navigating the New Landscape

On the other side of the gateway, the landscape shifts. It is not necessarily easier, nor is it without its own unique challenges and demands. However, it is organized around acceptance rather than resistance, trust rather than management, and the quiet wisdom of the journey rather than the relentless anxiety of the destination.

The framework of (Place in Time and Time in Place) PIT and TIP carries significant relevance in the aftermath of surrender. The PIT, as described in previous chapters, is the season of dormant potential: the time of formation, interior work, and the preparation for something that is not ready to emerge. The TIP is the season of active potential: when the formation has done its work and the time is right for what has been growing in the darkness to finally break into the light.

Much of the frustration that drives the need for control is the frustration of attempting to force TIP before the PIT has completed its work. The seed pushed too early from the ground, harvesting the fruit before it ripens. Understanding that the season will turn in its own time, and that the ripening cannot be accelerated by impatience or force.

The wisdom of aging demonstrates the necessity of a longer perspective that comes from having watched enough cycles of loss and renewal to trust the patterns that surrender eventually delivers. The urgency of youth, which experiences every delay as a threat and loss as potentially permanent, gives way to the deeper patience of someone who has learned, through accumulated experience, that endings consistently prepare the ground for beginnings that could not have arrived any sooner.

To live in the aftermath of surrender is a faith walk in a new direction. One that is guided not by the management of outcomes but by the deep, abiding acceptance of what is revealed. In this freedom, we find that the liberation of energy once consumed by resistance is now available for meaningful engagement with the life that is here, rather than the life that was supposed to be.

This freedom allows us to love life in a unique way. The person who has surrendered the need to protect themselves from loss is more open to love than before. They have learned, through the specific curriculum of their own grief and release, that love is worth the cost of living.

Control was never the source of safety
and surrender was never the loss of it.

Chapter Seventeen

Dreaming into Destiny

Unveiling God's Goodness, Mercy, and Blessings

The Guidepost of Divine Instruction

Dreams are among the oldest forms of divine communication known to humankind. These nocturnal narratives are symbolic stories sent to awaken our deeper awareness. They arrive in the hours when the waking mind has finally quieted enough for something truer to speak. Through dreams, the Spirit often bypasses our resistance and addresses the heart directly rarely permitted during the day.

To dismiss dreams as random neural noise is to overlook one of the most consistent and cross-culturally attested forms through which divine goodness has always shaped human journeys. To receive them as guidance, however, requires more than fascination. It requires spiritual attentiveness that most of us have never been taught.

Upon waking, rather than rushing immediately into the demands of the day, pause. Hold the impressions that remain in some of the images, emotions, and narrative fragments that linger at the edge of waking consciousness. Write them down, however incomplete or regardless of how they may appear. These fragments often carry wisdom whose meaning unfolds slowly, across days, months or in some cases of years.

Bring what you have received before the Divine in prayer, seeking illumination rather than mere interpretation. Interpretation is the work of the intellect, analyzing, comparing, and drawing conclusions. Illumination is something deeper. It is the quiet unveiling of meaning that emerges when the mind releases its demand to understand and becomes willing instead to listen, receive, and be taught. In the posture of openness, insight often arrives not as a conclusion, but as a truth being revealed. Apply what aligns with truth and peace. Allow action to confirm what revelation has suggested. And remain patient with the rest, knowing that not every dream arrives with its meaning already assembled. Some are seeds whose season has not yet come.

Dreams are not fortune-telling devices. They are invitations to participate in Divine creativity nudging us toward better choices, illuminating inner conflicts, reaffirming directions already impressed upon the spirit.

The Seeds of Divine Favor

God's goodness is dynamic, never dormant. It is the sustaining energy that orchestrates the rhythm of life from breath to breakthrough. This goodness is not merely what is given. It is God's essence expressed continuously in the fabric of a world and through humankind.

To perceive it requires the cultivation of an inner vision that has learned to notice grace in both the majestic and the mundane. A conversation that arrives bearing exactly the comfort needed. A provision that appears precisely the moment the resource runs out. A delay that, in retrospect, saved us from a disaster we never knew was coming. These are not coincidences dressed in spiritual language. They are the specific, ongoing expressions of our spiritual connections.

Within this field of goodness lie the seeds of divine favor. They are planted in moments of awareness when our deepest desires and God's intentions begin to harmonize. When the direction we sense is right and aligns briefly and beautifully, to be the same direction. Each seed represents potential: a lesson not yet learned, a calling not yet answered, an opportunity waiting for the right season and the seed planted in nutrient rich soil.

When dreams emerge during these seasons of readiness, they often carry coded affirmations encouraging perseverance, confirming direction, assuring that effort is required and the path is blessed. Through mindful engagement such as journaling, meditating, returning to the images with patience and openness is when these seeds are watered. Insight becomes an instruction. The nocturnal narrative joins the waking life, and together they move toward something neither could reach alone.

To live in awareness of divine goodness is to recognize that we are both recipients and participants. The honesty we practice, compassion we extend, and the integrity we maintain when no one is watching either nurtures or neglects the seeds of favor planted in us. When thought aligns with love and action mirrors truth, divine favor multiplies. Peace deepens. Creativity opens. Confidence roots itself in something that circumstances cannot erode. The soil of the soul becomes fertile ground for destiny that has been prepared for it.

The Desert Seasons

No journey of destiny unfolds without its deserts. Even those who walk in divine favor will encounter seasons of dryness. These intervals of testing arrive not as evidence of abandonment, but as invitations into a deeper and more enduring trust. These barren stretches of the path often feel empty at first, yet they serve as lessons where the soul learns what abundance alone cannot teach.

It is in these seasons that dependence deepens, humility takes root, and faith is refined. Not the faith that flourishes when every prayer appears answered, but the quieter and stronger faith that remains steadfast when evidence of progress has disappeared. In the desert, the soul learns to trust in God's presence. It is there in the absence of certainty that mercy performs some of its most transformative work.

Mercy, in its fullest meaning, is the sustaining compassion of a divine presence that keeps us steady while we wait for the promise while holding us in the dry seasons. To desire mercy is to admit, honestly and without shame, our need for divine companionship in patient waiting. It is recognizing that the season requires more than our own resources can provide.

Mercy, received this way, becomes a soothing balm. When doors close, it keeps bitterness from taking root. When confusion clouds the way forward, it clears our sight not by giving answers, but by restoring trust in the One who holds them. Through prayer, rest, and forgiving ourselves for what we did not yet know, mercy heals our perception and returns us to the quiet confidence that delay is not denial, but by design.

Prayer in desert seasons is transformative. It shifts from the steady, confident voice of someone who knows what to ask into a conversation in which slowly yields to something greater. This change is not comfortable, but it is necessary. As we pray, plead, and persevere, the Spirit quietly reshapes the motives beneath our requests, removing the fear and pride that distorts our desire until what remains is simpler, truer, and more aligned.

Faith, in this context, is not passive belief awaiting confirmation. It is disciplined confidence — the conscious choice to act as though Divine goodness is already at work even when visible evidence has not yet caught up to the reality. Faith measures progress not by sight but by surrender. It transforms the despair of the desert into expectancy, teaching us to interpret the dry season not as failure but as the particular form that preparation is taking at this particular moment in the journey.

The Harvest of Blessing

The harvest serves as a divine metaphor for completion. The manifestation of promises once hidden beneath soil and season, invisible to every eye except the one that planted and nurtured them. The harvest of blessing arrives not as a reward for perfection, but as the natural fruit of perseverance; it is the moment where preparation and providence finally converge in the fullness in its appointed time.

Patience prepares the ground for faith and the genuine gratitude of someone who begins to recognize the pattern: the seeds of divine favor ripening into visible fruit. Opportunities emerge. Relationships are restored. And the inner peace promised in the earliest chapters finally arrives not as a passing feeling, but as a steady foundation.

The truest measure of a harvest is not material abundance, but the wisdom it yields. Material gains may come and go; fortunes may rise and fall, but wisdom endures. It is a fruit that survives changing circumstances, remains untouched by reversals of fortune, and cannot be diminished by the passing of time.

Wisdom is the essence distilled from lived experiences. It is understanding refined through trial, serenity cultivated through surrender, and discernment forged in the unique curriculum of a life faithfully navigated. Every hardship endured, every lesson learned, and every season traversed contributes to its formation. Unlike possessions, achievements, or status, wisdom becomes part of the person who acquires it.

Of all the fruits produced by life's harvest, wisdom belongs most completely to the one who has grown it. It is also the fruit that is most easily shared. It can be offered freely to others without being diminished, illuminating their path while continuing to enrich the one who carries it. In this way, wisdom becomes both the inheritance of a life well-lived and a gift that extends far beyond the boundaries of one's own journey.

During harvest season divine communication often delivers a new sense of clarity. Dreams return with a precision that earlier seasons could not sustain. Guidance becomes less something to decipher and more something to recognize. It reveals itself through timing, through meaningful convergences, through doors that open and others that gently close, and through the unmistakable quality of peace that accompanies each decision along the path.

By this stage of the journey, faith itself has matured. It is no longer defined by the urgent need for answers or the pursuit of certainty. The soul has learned that divine guidance is not merely something to receive, but a presence in which to dwell. Faith evolves from asking to abiding. From the earnest petitions of one seeking direction to the settled confidence of one who has learned to live in communion. What was once sought in moments of crisis becomes a continuous awareness; a quiet companionship woven into the ordinary rhythms of life.

In this season, trust no longer depends upon constant reassurance. The relationship itself amplifies reassurance. The soul rests more easily in mystery because it has come to recognize the character of the Divine who guides it. And from that place of abiding, guidance flows with a naturalness that feels less like receiving instructions and more like walking in step with a wisdom that has been present all along.

Blessings are the outward flow of inward alignment. When mercy has softened the places that were rigid and faith has strengthened what was fragile, we become conduits of divine generosity, and not accumulators of gifts. Our words carry healing, and our presence offers something to the people around us that cannot be manufactured or taught. Our work has an impact that outlasts the effort that produced it. The purpose of blessing is not possession but distribution. The joy of sharing what grace has given us is itself the fullness of the harvest.

Divine Appointment

I have lived in this process not as a spectator of spiritual principles, but as a student and, at times, an unwilling subject.

In 1985, a dream arrived carrying four specifics: military service, a relocation to California, a dark cloud over my city, and a meeting with a woman named Darla. Each unfolded in its season not through my manipulation of circumstances, but through the quiet orchestration of a design I could not have constructed and would not have chosen.

The dream was a seed of divine favor, planted long before its meaning could be fully understood. It became my first lesson in the language of trust that Divine goodness often speaks before the path is visible. That mercy sustains the soul through the long interval between promise and fulfillment, and that wisdom is not merely the ability to wait, but the capacity to recognize the answer when it arrives in a form different than imagined.

Years later, when I arrived at the season of surrender described in the previous chapter, I prayed for a prayer that was simpler and more honest than most I had managed before: if companionship is meant for me, let it find me in your season, not mine. That prayer was the tilling of the soil and the conscious release of the timeline I had been managing and while releasing the grip and opening my hands.

The answer came on a shuttle bus at O'Hare Airport, disguised as the most ordinary of encounters. A brief conversation. A shared laugh. A business card offered to a potential first client. Nothing that would have been registered as significant in any other context. Divine goodness was already at work in those few minutes weaving together threads of connection that reached back generations before either of us was born.

When I later visited the home of the woman who would become my wife, her grandfather opened the door and looked at me with a familiarity I had done nothing to earn. Within moments, we discovered that he had known my grandparent's decades earlier. Their lives had intersected long before either of us had been born, woven together through shared history, migration, and neighborhood in a world that existed before our stories had even begun.

Standing there on that threshold, I felt the quiet weight of something sacred. It was as if an unseen thread had stretched across generations, connecting lives separated by time yet bound together in ways neither family could have anticipated. In that moment, I understood something about destiny that I had only partially grasped before. Destiny is rarely random. It is profoundly relational. What often may be dismissed as a coincidence may be something far more intentional.

Our story became the living embodiment of the very principles I had spent years learning through the PIT and the seasons of formation that preceded it. It was faith exercised in the dry seasons when evidence was scarce, and trust was all that remained. It was mercy received in moments of failure, weakness, and immaturity. It was a blessing fulfilled not as a prize but as a covenant to be stewarded.

What emerged was a relationship whose depth, resilience, and enduring quality bore witness to something greater than human planning. It testified the precision of a divine design that had been quietly shaping two separate lives long before they converged. Through unseen preparations, unexpected detours, seasons of waiting, and lessons neither of us would have chosen for ourselves, a larger purpose had been at work.

Looking back, it became clear that we had not simply found one another. We had been formed for one another, separately and then together, by a wisdom whose care extended far beyond what either of us could see at the time.

The Illuminated Path

Life unfolds as a continual invitation to awareness. Every person encountered, every challenge endured, every loss absorbed and every breakthrough received adds another level of instruction to the journey. When we cultivate the discipline of mindfulness by listening before reacting, observing before judging, pausing in the space between stimulus and response long enough to ask what this moment is teaching. We begin to see how goodness detours into design. Distractions will always compete for the attention that the illuminated path requires. Faithful living requires disciplined perception to recognize that these distractions are competing for the very quality of attention the journey truly demands.

The illuminated path is not the path of perfection. It is the path of orientation and the steady turning of the soul toward the light through seasons of uncertainty, confusion, and difficulty. Along this path, certain truths become unmistakable. A soul that loses its compassion gradually loses its clarity, for love is not separate from wisdom but one of its highest expressions. A life that pursues advancement without humility creates motion but not meaning; noise, but not insight. Humility keeps perception clear. Compassion keeps the heart aligned. Together, they preserve the conditions under which true discernment can flourish.

The freedom described throughout these pages has never been the freedom to do whatever one desires. It is something deeper and more enduring: the freedom to love generously, to create responsibly, to serve sincerely, and to participate fully in the unfolding of one's purpose. It is the freedom that emerges when the soul is no longer governed by fear, bitterness, resentment, or the endless demands of the self.

This is the atmosphere in which destiny breathes. It is the climate in which wisdom matures, relationships deepen, and purpose finds expression. It is not a destination reached once and for all, but a way of traveling in continued alignment with the light that guides, sustains, and calls each life into alignment with its purpose.

Destiny is the gradual unveiling of divine instruction written into our lives long before we were able to understand it. We begin to see specific moments of clarity that every experience was part of the curriculum of our becoming. Every joy and every loss, every season of waiting and every test endured, even failures carried some form of instruction. All of it was preparation. None of it was wasted.

God's goodness appears in the second chances we do not deserve. Mercy appears in every recovery from the failures we did not survive alone. Blessing appears in each breath that keeps us going in the ordinary, unremarkable continuation of a life that has been accompanied every moment by a presence more faithful than our attention deserves.

Wisdom is the final harvest not the mere accumulation of knowledge, but the deep comprehension that transforms experience into guidance for others. It is the clarity that allows us to live not only blessed but beneficial, turning personal testimony into communal teaching. It turns the specific, costly, and irreplaceable curriculum of a single life into a light for those walking in the same terrain, offering them the vital assurance that it is possible to reach the other side.

To live in destiny is to live alert trusting the process, practicing gratitude, and remaining teachable when the lesson arrives in a form that pride might refuse. God grants us enough time, grace, and mercy to complete the assignment set before us. Each sunrise is a continuation of that instruction; each day is another page of the curriculum that began before we were born and will not be finished until we have given away everything we were meant to give. For in doing so, you become the evidence of God's goodness, mercy, and blessing alive in the world.

The dream was always a seed,
the journey was always the soil,
and the harvest was always coming.

Chapter Eighteen

Choosing Life

Navigating the Darkness of Suicidal Thoughts

Choosing Life

If you are reading this chapter from inside the PIT, I want to say something to you before anything else: you are not broken. You are not beyond restoration. What you are experiencing is real, and it is serious, and it deserves to be met with honesty rather than reassurance that papers over the depth of what you are carrying.

This chapter will not offer you easy comfort. It will offer you something I believe is more valuable: the truth that others have stood where you are standing, have felt what you are feeling, and have found not without cost the of struggle but a path back to life. That path is real. It is available. And the fact that you cannot see it from where you are does not mean it does not exist.

Choosing life is not a test you must pass. It is not a performance of strength or a demonstration of faith. It is a quiet return to alignment repeatedly, in ordinary moments as much as the dramatic ones. The invitation to choose life will come again. When it does, it will not arrive as a verdict of your worth. It will come in a moment of truth. A breath. A single next step and that is enough to begin.

You are not broken. You are not beyond restoration. You are learning at great cost and with great courage how to live aligned. And in that alignment, however distant it feels; there is peace.

Understanding the Descent

The descent into suicidal thoughts is more often a gradual erosion of a darkening of the inner landscape that happens so slowly that the person inside it may not notice how far the light has receded until the darkness feels encompassing. Understanding the why behind these thoughts is not an academic exercise. It is an act of compassion toward yourself and toward anyone you are trying to reach.

Experiencing suicidal thoughts is not a sign of weakness or a moral failure, nor is it evidence that the person experiencing them is less worthy of life, less resilient, or less deserving of hope than anyone else. Rather, it is a signal of profound distress and a cry from the mind, body, and spirit that the burden of suffering is too much to carry.

Suicidal thoughts are often the mind's attempt to find relief when pain has become overwhelming. They communicate that something within is exhausted, wounded, and in need of care. The presence of these thoughts does not define a person. It reveals only that they have been carrying more than they can sustain alone.

If you find yourself at this point in the journey, do not turn away. Stay with me. Keep reading. The fact that you are here means that some part of you is still searching, still listening, still hoping that another way forward exists.

Honor that part. Hold on to it. The pages ahead were written for moments such this and for people like you.

The Weight Behind the Thoughts

Mental illness is among the most significant contributors to suicidal thoughts. Depression, bipolar disorder, severe anxiety, and trauma disorders are conditions that do not simply make life harder. They distort the perception of life itself, creating a cognitive and emotional environment in which worthlessness feels like truth, hopelessness feels like accuracy, and the pain feels not only unbearable but permanent.

The mind under this kind of pressure is not thinking clearly. It is thinking from within a state of mental illness, and the thoughts it produces however compelling are not reliable guides to reality. One must also consider whether the suicidal thoughts are attributed to prescription medication as a stated side-effect.

The weight of pain and loss compounds this. The accumulated grief of losses not fully mourned. The unresolved problems that have been carried for too long. The guilt that has hardened into a belief that the person is fundamentally at fault for their own suffering. The shame that whispers you are a burden to the people who love you and that whisper is always false and almost always believed. These burdens are real. Their weight is real. And the suffering they produce is not a weakness. It is the honest response of a human being carrying more than they should.

The mind rationalizes a way to escape by solving an overwhelming problem by choosing to end life. It promises an end to the pain. And because the pain is real, the logic feels real too. This is why it must be named honestly rather than dismissed. The person in its grip is not irrational. They are in pain. The compassionate response to pain is never dismissal. It is presence, witness, and the quiet, patient insistence that another way exists.

The Dangerous Crossroads

There is a specific and dangerous escalation that can occur when suicidal thoughts move from the abstract to the concrete. When the mind seeks relief from unbearable pain, begins to consider not just whether but when, where and how. This progression is a crisis, and it requires immediate response. Not judgment or shame, just a response.

The inner turmoil of this stage is unlike anything else in human experience. The mind becomes a relentless engine of activity, generating thoughts that race without rest and questions that seem to multiply faster than answers can solve. Every disappointment is magnified. Every mistake becomes evidence of inadequacy. Every setback appears to confirm the fear that things will never improve.

Perhaps most tragically, the very creative faculty that makes us capable of innovation, imagination, and hope begins to turn against itself. The mind's extraordinary capacity to envision possibilities no longer creates pathways toward the future. Instead, it becomes preoccupied with constructing an eject button from the present. The same creativity that might otherwise imagine healing, growth, and new beginnings is recruited into the service of ending pain. The imagination ceases to ask, "What could my life become?" and begins asking, "How can I make this stop?"

This reversal is one of the cruelest features of profound despair. The mind that was designed to create, build, dream, and discover becomes consumed with finding an exit rather than a way forward. Yet even in this distorted state, something important remains true: the imagination itself is not the enemy. The very capacity that has been turned toward escape can, in time, be reclaimed and redirected toward healing, purpose, and the creation of a future not yet visible from within the darkness.

The battle for self-control in this stage is exhausting in ways that people who have not experienced it cannot fully imagine. The desire to end the suffering collides with the instinct for survival in a war of attrition that depletes every resource. What is most important to understand about this stage is that the person inside it is not beyond reach. They are not beyond help. But they need that help now, not later. The courage required to reach out in this moment is enormous. It is also the most important act available.

If you are in this stage, if the thoughts have moved from abstract to concrete, if you are planning, please reach out. To a trusted person, counselor, doctor, crisis line. The fact that you are still reading means the part of you that want to live is still present. Honor that part. It is telling you the truth.

The Pivotal Decision

Yet somewhere within the darkness, however faint; a flicker of light remains. It may not feel powerful or hopeful. It is simply a small but persistent impulse toward life as a quiet counterweight to the immense gravity of despair.

This is the pivotal moment of the journey. Not the dramatic disappearance of suffering. Not the sudden arrival of optimism or certainty. Rather, it is a quiet but courageous decision to move one step away from the edge. A decision made not because the pain has ended, but because some part of the soul, however wounded, remains unwilling to surrender its claim in the future.

The choice is often less dramatic than it looks. It may be a single phone call, and honest sentence, accepting help, or simply deciding to make it through one more day. Yet within that small act is extraordinary courage. It is the moment of life fragile and trembling, choosing life once again.

This decision does not require certainty of feeling better. It does not require believing that life will be worth living. It requires only the willingness to postpone that decision at this moment but choose to remain. And then choose it again in the next moment. And the one after that. Choosing life is not one single decision. It is built through small, steady choices to stay until choosing life becomes more natural, and the pull toward the edge grows weaker.

The body and spirit carry this battle together. The body, which is a temporary vessel for a life of uncommon significance, signals its distress in physical ways such as disrupted sleep, loss of an appetite, and exhaustion that is more than physical. The spirit, in its deepest nature, resists this premature ending of what was given to it as a gift for a specific purpose. To end a life before that purpose is fulfilled is, in the language of the spirit, a loss that extends beyond the individual, a light extinguished before it could illuminate the world in its own unique way.

The Witness

I want to be honest with you about where this chapter comes from. It is not written from a safe distance. It is written from the inside of the experience, and from beside the people I have loved who walked this road.

Uncle Larry

Larry was my uncle, and he died by suicide. I wrote about his death in Chapter 11. When the news reached me in the Bahrain desert, his final words to me "I love you" still carried the same weight they do today.

Our conversation pertained to the construction work I was doing in the Middle East. I thanked him for the experience I gained from him exposing me to new construction projects for KFC, Pizza Hut, and Taco Bell restaurants. I didn't know it at the time, but he was struggling financially. The 2008, financial crisis had devastated his business, and the complications from anti-depressive medication was too much for him to bare.

His death was not something I could have prevented, and over the years I have had to come to terms with that painful truth. Yet the loss remains one of the most formative experiences of my life not only because of the grief it carried, but because of what it revealed.

It taught me about the hidden nature of suffering. About the burdens, people carry behind composed faces and ordinary conversations. About the silence that so often surrounds profound emotional pain, allowing it to deepen unnoticed and unwitnessed. Some struggles are visible to the world, but others unfold entirely in private, concealed behind habit, responsibility, and the appearance of being fine.

What remains with me most is the realization that much of this suffering is endured alone when it was never meant to be. Human beings are not designed to carry unbearable pain in isolation. We require presence, understanding, and witness. We need someone willing to step into the darkness with us long enough to remind us that we do not have to face it alone. His loss impressed that truth upon me in a way no lesson ever could, and it continues to shape how I understand grief, compassion, and the responsibility we have to one another.

Larry's death is one of the reasons this chapter exists. Not as an explanation, but as a refusal to maintain the silence that may have contributed to his isolation. He deserved to be known in his isolated pain. So do you.

David

David was my neighbor when I was in high school. He was in twenties who drove the prettiest cars, had the prettiest girl friends. He was a very popular guy with many people wanting to hang out with him. There was a dark side to him as he was very violent and sometimes uncontrollable and would beat up his mother. Sometimes, she would take refuge in our home. It was drugs and alcohol abuse which prevented him from living another life.

I have witnessed the devastation that suicide leaves behind. It creates a kind of grief that carries questions that linger long after the funeral has ended and answers that never fully arrive. Those who remain are left to navigate not only the loss itself, but the haunting uncertainty that accompanies it. The conversations replayed, signs overlooked, and the endless search for understanding in places that can no longer be found.

An absence of this kind does not simply remove a person from a family; it reshapes the emotional landscape of everyone who remains. Relationships change. Memories take on new meanings. Milestones are marked by the awareness of who is missing from them. The loss becomes woven into the story of the family, not as a chapter that closes, but as a reality that continues to echo through the years. The pain may soften with time, but the imprint remains, altering the lives of those left behind.

Tyrone

My cousin's struggle with suicidal thoughts wasn't widely known. My aunt told me to check in on him, but he was never available. She told me he had attempted to commit suicide but failed. Several weeks later he chose to end his life. Regretfully, the darkness taught me the profound limits of what one person can offer to another in crisis, and the equally profound importance of simply refusing to look away.

The family carried the weight. The aftermath of a suicide is not only the loss of a person. It is the loss of the future that person would have inhabited, and the specific, irreplaceable contribution they would have made to the lives of everyone that loved them, even his children.

When I reflect on what is truly at stake in choosing life, I often think of those who remain. The decision to stay is never only about ourselves. It is also about the family, friends, partners, children, and loved ones whose lives are bound to ours and who would carry the weight of that loss long after the moment had passed.

In seasons of profound despair, suffering can narrow one's field of vision until the pain feels entirely personal and inescapable. Yet beyond that pain exists a wider circle of lives that would be forever altered by an absence of that kind. The choice to remain is, in part, a choice made on behalf of those relationships. It is an acknowledgment that our lives belong not only to us, but also to a network of connections, memories, responsibilities, and love that extends far beyond what we can always see in our darkest moments.

These three men is the reason why this chapter is necessary. Suicide is not an abstraction. It is the specific loss of specific people whose presence mattered and whose absence leaves a specific shape in the lives of everyone who knew them, especially me.

Choosing the Path Toward Life

The decisive moment comes differently for each person. For some, it arrives as clarity that reveals a single step forward when none seems possible. For others, it emerges more quietly through the steady accumulation of small choices, each insignificant on its own, until a new direction forms and a life begins to change.

What matters is not how the moment arrives, but how we respond. Transformation rarely requires a full map of the future. It asks only for the courage to take the next visible step. The mind longs for certainty, wanting proof that the path ahead will lead somewhere worthwhile before committing to it. Yet healing rarely arrives with a complete map. The way forward emerges through motion itself, each step uncovering a little more of the path that could not be seen while standing still.

The invitation is not to wait until every question is answered or every doubt resolved. It is to act on the light already given. Every meaningful journey begins the same way: not with full understanding, but with the willingness to move forward before full understanding arrives.

Reconnecting and Redirecting

Reconnection after a decisive moment is rarely dramatic. More often, it takes shape in ordinary life, and that is where healing begins. Activities like visiting the zoo, walking through a park, or calling a missed friend are not trivial. Returning to a simple meal, a routine, or a pleasure that the darkness once made inaccessible is a profound victory. These are the deliberate, specific choices of a person who has decided, in the most fundamental sense, to remain present and engaged with the life that is here.

An honest recognition of how one's absence would affect those who love them can become powerful anchors in the earliest stages of choosing life. Not as a source of guilt, but as a reminder of connection. It is the realization that no life exists in isolation, that each person is woven into a network of relationships whose significance often extends far beyond what they can see in moments of despair.

To remember this is to remember that one's presence matters. It carries weight and shapes the lives of others in ways both visible and unseen. There are specific people whose stories have become intertwined with your own.

People who would feel the loss not as an abstract tragedy, but as a deeply personal absence that could never be fully replaced.

The day after a crisis is a fragile place. The immediate pressure may have eased, but the underlying pain and the ingrained patterns that produced the crisis have not disappeared. This is the moment for gentleness because you survived, and recognizing the courage it required to choose life when the alternative felt more manageable. Treat yourself the way you would treat someone you loved who had just survived something almost unsurvivable. With care and patience, without demanding immediate strength.

The days of remembrance like anniversaries and certain seasons may trigger emotional responses that return the darkness with renewed intensity are real. Honoring them is not the same as being defeated by them. It is the acknowledgment that the struggle was real, that the path required courage, and that the person who walked it is stronger than the darkness that tried to imprison them.

Your Story Is Not Over

I want to end this chapter and this book by speaking directly to the person who may be reading it from the darkest place they have ever inhabited.

Your story is not over. I know that this may be the least convincing sentence you have read today, because from inside the darkness the story feels very much like it is ending. But the feeling that the story is ending is a symptom of the darkness, not a reliable report on the actual state of reality. The darkness lies about this. It has always lied about this. Every person who has found their way through and there are millions, and their testimony is consistent will tell you the same thing: the darkness can be overcome, and you'll need to take the steps necessary to climb out of the PIT when you are ready.

The journey of this book has been, from its first page, about the possibility of transformation and the process of human struggle. Every chapter has been testimony to the same truth: that what the darkness calls the end is almost never the end. It is, far more often, the threshold of something that the darkness cannot yet allow you to see.

You have arrived at this page, which means that despite everything you have endured, some part of you still wants to live. That part may feel small. It may feel fragile, exhausted, and overshadowed by pain. But do not mistake its size for its significance. It is not a trivial thing. It is not an afterthought.

It is everything.

It is the part of you that continues searching when surrender is easier. The part that continues listening when despair insists there is nothing left to hear. The part that has not completely relinquished its claim not on the future but in it. The fact that you are reading these words is evidence that this part remains alive within you.

Choosing life is not a single decision
it is the hopeful revelation of what's coming

www.ingramcontent.com/pod-product-compliance
Lightning Source LLC
LaVergne TN
LVHW011811200926
848484LV00005B/1150
* 9 7 9 8 9 9 6 5 4 6 3 1 2 *